# THE BOOK OF LIGHT

All proceeds from the sale of this book go directly to
The Medical Foundation For the Care of Victims of Torture

*Caring for victims of torture*
**MEDICAL FOUNDATION**

# THE BOOK OF LIGHT

Waterstone's Collection of Writing for
The Medical Foundation For the Care of Victims of Torture

WATERSTONE'S

Published in association
with Random House

Published by Random House 1998

2 4 6 8 10 9 7 5 3

Selection copyright © Waterstone's Booksellers Ltd 1998
Introduction copyright © The Medical Foundation
For the Care of Victims of Torture 1998

Page 98 constitutes an extension of this copyright page

The right of the contributors to be identified as the
authors of this work has been asserted by them in accordance
with the Copyright, Designs and Patents Act, 1988

First published in Great Britain by
Random House in association with Waterstone's, 1998

Random House UK Limited
Random House, 20 Vauxhall Bridge Road, London SW1V 2SA

Random House Australia (Pty) Limited
20 Alfred Street, Milsons Point, Sydney,
New South Wales 2061, Australia

Random House New Zealand Limited
18 Poland Road, Glenfield
Auckland 10, New Zealand

Random House South Africa (Pty) Limited
Endulini, 5A Jubilee Road, Parktown 2193, South Africa

Random House UK Limited Reg. No. 954009

A CIP catalogue record for this book
is available from the British Library

ISBN 0 09 928869 9

Papers used by Random House UK Ltd are natural,
recyclable products made from wood grown in
sustainable forests. The manufacturing processes
conform to the environmental regulations of the
country of origin

Typeset in 10½/12 Sabon by
MATS, Southend-on-Sea, Essex
Printed and bound in Great Britain by
Cox & Wyman Ltd, Reading, Berkshire

# The Medical Foundation For the Care of Victims of Torture

## Care is our Mission

During the year over 2,500 victims of torture and systematic violence will make their way to our overcrowded offices in a side street of Kentish Town. At this traditionally festive this time of year their numbers are not diminished; indeed, our joyful celebrations make their plight all the more wretched.

The Medical Foundation exists to enable survivors of torture and organised violence to engage in a healing process to assert their own human dignity and worth. We advocate respect for human rights and our concern for the health and well-being of survivors of torture and their families. We provide them with medical and social care, practical assistance, and psychological and physical therapy. Besides this individual treatment, dozens of our clients, including adolescents and children, participate in the 12 therapy groups that offer activities in story-telling, art, gardening, cooking, dance movement and traditional discussion.

These torture survivors have experienced the unimaginable: severe beatings, electric shock, falaka (beating on the soles of the feet), prolonged suspension in contorted positions, mock executions, sexual abuse and rape (both male and female), sleep deprivation and so on. The catalogue of violations is as long as it is inhuman.

Founded in 1986, the Medical Foundation is an independent charity (charity number 1000340). It is the only organisation of its kind in the United Kingdom. The Medical Foundation is staffed by more than a hundred volunteers and employees, including medical, clinical and professional support staff. Essential to our services is our team of interpreters, who facilitate communication between staff and clients in some 25 languages.

The medical doctors document torture survivors' cases in detail, sometimes patiently spending hours with an individual client over more than one session. To document torture and ill-treatment, both physical and psychological, Foundation doctors write over 600 forensic medical reports a year. Foundation counsellors write many more reports about clients who suffer long-term psychological or social disturbances as a result of torture. Our doctors also find that the very giving of testimony by the torture survivor – the exhaustingly detailed record itself – often becomes part of the treatment.

Our psychiatrists deal with the small number of survivors where there is a formal mental illness, a possible need for medication or a risk of suicide. In addition, all the doctors liaise with the client's GP or with hospital specialists to obtain the best possible care for the client, whether the NHS or at the Foundation.

Foundation psychotherapists work with clients to help them address their losses and integrate them into their new society. This is a partnership, with the therapist holding and supporting, perhaps over several years, as the client learns to cope with past and present pain. Unlike classical psychotherapy, this support includes help with practicalities and asylum issues. All our caseworkers have a counselling background so even practical problems are addressed with an understanding of torture, exile and the great loss of separation from family and homeland.

The Foundation's physiotherapist and our team of ten volunteer complementary therapists strive to help clients overcome their physical problems and regain control over their bodies – always using techniques that avoid pain or any hint of threat. Again, the specialist nature of this team is significant. At the Foundation they can give all the time needed; they have access to interpreters and to colleagues who are knowledgeable about the client's country of origin and cultural background. Nowhere is our holistic approach required more than with children and families, who often have quite different needs from single adults.

In all this work we rely utterly on the support of individuals like yourself.

If you would like to support this work directly kindly contact us at the Medical Foundation, Star House, 104-108 Grafton Road, Kentish Town, London NW4 5BD or call our freephone number 0800 068 7112.

Dr Helen Bamber OBE

# CONTENTS

# Nicholas Allan

## NATIVITY GAME

# Louis de Bernières

## OUR LADY OF BEAUTY

THE SEPULCHRE WAS situated in the communal graveyard of Santa Madre de Jesus in the province of Santander. This graveyard was, on account of its location upon the side of the volcano, almost unique in that everybody was buried upright and above ground, enclosed by four slabs glued poorly together by a pinkish mortar ground from tufa and mixed with lime and water. Often this mortar would crack, and crumble away, so that by the light of a match or a taper the local children could peer into the darkness of the tombs and wonder at what they saw. Inside, draped with spiders' webs and often with snakes coiled around them, they would behold the mummified ancestors of the village; they would discern wisps of gossamer-like hair sprouting thinly from yellow scalps so shrunken that through the rents one could see white bone. There were shrivelled lips drawn back in the parody of smiles and snarls, and one could wobble the teeth in their sockets by poking at them with a stick.

Sometimes one could see a cloth around the jaw, knotted at the top of the head to prevent the mouth from falling open, and some of the corpses had coins in the eyes for the payment of the boatman who ferries souls across the last waters. Occasionally, for a reason unknown, the corpse's head would have turned so that when one peeped through the chinks one's heart would leap to the throat with the horror of discovering that the cadaver was staring back as though it had been waiting there for years for a glimpse of the light in living eyes. There was one child in the pueblo who, having seen this, was pursued relentlessly by nightmares until one night she ran

3

shrieking from her father's house and was lost in the maw of an opportunistic jaguar. Her grave is out on the edge of the cemetery, and is so small that one can lift off the lid at the top and see the pathetic pile of scored bones held together with the leather thongs of ligament and cartilage. Sometimes her father lifts it off himself to place orchids and blossoms of bougainvillaea within, and he raises the skull in his hands and talks to it, kissing the lips and tenderly arranging what is left of the long dark hair. In this way he overcomes the tragedy of separation and accustoms himself to death.

We are a village accustomed to death. Every generation has borne witness to a new devastation. In my grandfather's time there was the plague of cholera that swept away all of his relatives, and the village was so cruelly emptied that he had to marry somebody from another place. In my father's time there was the violence, when there was one band of political guerrillas after another coming through, raping, robbing and murdering, starting and continuing vendettas that flare up all over again to this very day. In my village no one votes in elections any more because of the memory of what outrages ensue from political idealism; when the communists tried to start a *foco* here we gave them away to the army, and then we got rid of the army by telling them that there were more communists towards San Isidro. We don't want any politics any more, and, if we voted, it would be a vote to be left alone.

In my own time we had the whooping cough that carried away one half of the children here and left so many empty cradles and broken hearts, and there was the avalanche when the south escarpment of the volcano broke away and flattened the end of the village where the brothel was. They say it was a judgement of God upon a house of infamy, but it carried away a good many fine men and women in addition to the revellers, not all of whom were very bad in any case. I might add that many of the whores survived, and that one of the dead was the priest, who had gone there to preach against the immoralities. It is because of the illogicality of God that around here we still worship the *orishas*, whom we can at least understand.

Above all, it is our cemetery that accustoms us to death. We grow up with our dead still visible amongst us, and one of them in particular. His name is Don Salvador, and he came here as a missionary about one hundred and fifty years ago. He lived here for forty years amongst us and had many fine children by various women; they say he was still a fine seducer even in his seventies, and when he died we made him a saint. It was not only out of gratitude that he had saved us from the damnation of the hell of the heathens, but also because he taught us so many things. He instructed us in writing and reading, he taught us Spanish, he taught us how to build bridges supported upon columns, and he taught us the art of making love. Before he came it was forbidden to make love in any position except with the man on top, but he instructed the local women in the use of the tongue and in the differing possibilities for positions. He taught that if God had proscribed these positions He would have constructed our bodies in such a way that they would have been impossible to perform, and very soon the old ways were abandoned. It is because of him that I am called Dominico.

But the principal reason why we made him a saint was that he was so fertile. We remember not only his many children and his bull's appetite for love, but we have been told by our grandparents that wherever he passed the flowers burst into bloom, the crops burgeoned, the trees grew heavy with fruit, and women and animals grew heavy with the unborn.

So when he died they never sealed up his tomb, but only placed the slab in front of it, in a groove that was chiselled out of the rock. The path to his resting place is worn smooth by those who have crawled to it on hands and knees to beg for children. One would slide the stone away and kiss his feet and his hands, begging his intercession with Our Lady of Conception. A garland of flowers would be always upon his head, and, despite the temptation to steal parts of him as holy relics, I have to say that nobody ever did, and he is still intact to this day. As a man there are things to which ordinarily I would not admit, but such is my devotion to Don Salvador that I state that it was he who cured me of my impotence with my wife, and I know many others for whom he has done the same, whose names I will not tell you in case it brings them shame.

In addition to Don Salvador's continued presence amongst us in his tomb, we carry him upon a litter around our fields twice a year when we do our planting. We sing hymns and songs, and we throw jugs of water on the ground, and it must be said that despite all the disasters we have suffered in the past, our crops, our animals, and our women have never failed us, except for the time when the new priest forbade us to perform the ceremony, saying that it was a pagan sacrilege. Nowadays nobody pays any attention to the new priest, and not just because of this.

Don José always contradicted the teaching of Don Salvador. He has even told us that Don Salvador must have been an impostor and an Antichrist. Don Jose wants us to be ashamed of our bodies and to go back to the practice of making love furtively in only one position, he wants us to stop using herbs to prevent unwanted pregnancies, and he wants to frighten us with stories about infernos of fire when we are dead. But we remember the teaching of Don Salvador which have been passed down to us, and we argue with Don José, saying that we have been told about God being a God of Love. When we pass Don José in the street we say, 'Be joyful in the Lord,' and his face just grows more sorrowful. We do not like to see a man so lonely, but that is the price of his perversity.

It happened one evening that there was an earthquake. It was not a serious one, even though it seemed terrifying at the time. There was a distant rumble like thunder, and everything started to shake and sway. In my hut the tin mug slid off the shelf and fell on to my wife, and the bell in the porch of the church began to ring on its own. Some of the animals panicked, and there was a bull who escaped from his corral and ended up entangled in the creepers at the edge of the forest. Everybody ran into the street, and most of us could not keep our balance, so we all fell over. Old Aldonaldo remained in his hammock smoking a *puro* and laughing at us, and he seemed to be the only stationary object in a world that had become as restless as the sea. He was calling out 'Ay, ay, ay' and enjoying every minute of it.

As it was the dry season, a great cloud of dust got shaken up, and we all got covered from head to toe in white dust. We were all coughing and falling about when Don José ran out of his house crying out, 'Repent, repent, the Kingdom of God is at hand. Woe to the inhabiters of the earth and of the sea, for the devil is come down unto you, having great wrath, because he knoweth that he hath but a short time.' No one was more disappointed than Don José to discover afterwards that there had been no damage to speak of.

In fact the only damage was to the cemetery, where the slabs in the front of the tombs had in most cases fallen away. In some of them the bodies had fallen out forwards and were splayed upon the ground like withered drunkards or like the casualties of a battle, but in most of them the dead were still upright.

We wandered about the cemetery awestruck. The corpses seemed to be leaning casually against the sides of their habitations, and despite their mummification, their yellowness, the transparency of their skin, and the whiteness of their bones, they seemed extraordinarily full of life, all except the recent corpses, which reeked horribly and dripped with a foul slime whose colour and odour comes back to me in bad dreams. We put the slabs back on those ones first, partly because of the offence to relatives, partly because of the stink, and partly because the vultures were showing an interest. Afterwards they perched forlornly on top of the graves, reminding me of how I felt when I could not crack a Brazil nut as a child.

Seeing the corpses brought the village back to its history. There were people there that had been all but forgotten, but now the living were wandering amongst them, recognising shreds of clothing, characteristic missing teeth, seeing the machete cuts of old murders, the broken bones of accidents. We were saying, 'Ay, that is Alfonso who lived by the river, who got bitten by the mad dog and who was in love with Rosalita,' and 'Ay, ay, there is Mahoma, who arrived from nowhere with his strange religion and took four wives, and :here is the holy book written in squiggles that he carried about with him and that he read from the back to the front,' and 'Look, this is Saba who was so beautiful that two men killed themselves out of love for her, and then she took up with Rafael who had only one arm.' It made many old folk happy to see their old friends again.

But one man was more strangely affected. In the oldest part of the cemetery a grave had opened, the identity of whose occupant nobody could fathom, and who was a miracle.

She had her eyes closed and she was very beautiful. People nowadays when they tell this story always say that she was in a perfect state and that she was as fresh as the day before she died. They will tell you that her lips were as moist as if she had just eaten a mango, and that she smelled of flowers and vanilla, but that is not exactly how I remember it.

I recall that her lips were dry, as they are when one wakes on a hot morning, and that she smelled of a house that has been shut up and never cleaned for years. People will tell you that her limbs were supple and full, whereas I recall them having the stiffness of an old lady. Otherwise, what they will tell you is mostly true.

I suppose it is possible that two centuries of death might have turned a dark woman white, but it seemed to us that she was a white lady because her skin was white like the flesh of a cassava, she had restrained lips, and her hair, although it was black, was very long and straight. Also she was tall, and so she could not have been an Indian woman. She was clothed in a kind of textile that we had never seen before; it was very finely woven, and although it was now a yellow colour and crumbled to the touch, it had obviously been very rich. About her waist she wore a red sash, and on her feet were black slippers embroidered in gold wire.

We accepted her mysterious presence and her lunar beauty as a miracle, but without too much excitement, since this is, as everyone knows, a land where anything is possible and everything has happened at one time or another. We made her a saint, like Don Salvador, and we made a groove at the front of her tomb so that the door could be slid aside, with the idea that our women could pray to her for their beauty and for that of their daughters, that it might last for ever. We called her Nuestra Señora de la Hermosura, and it seemed reasonable to include her in our history as the favourite wife of Don Salvador.

But my brother Manolito was never the same man again. I was with him when he first saw her, and I remember vividly how strange his reaction was. He was a dark man, but he turned pale. He caught his breath, and he told me later that truly his heart ceased to beat for a second or two, so greatly did it leap in his chest. He looked at me with a wild expression, and then made a kind of expansive gesture, as though he were showing me into a richly appointed apartment. 'Fijate,' he said, inviting me to look, as though I had not already seen.

'She is very beautiful,' I said, but he looked at me again as though I were stupid. 'She is exquisite,' he replied; it was the first time I had ever heard him use a word as poetic as 'exquisita', and I laughed at him. 'Don't fall in love with a corpse,' I said, 'she will be very boring in bed.'

Manolito seemed to take the comment seriously. He put his hands together, as in an attitude of prayer, and said 'She is lovely beyond the dreams of flesh. One could love her in the spirit and be satisfied.'

'You are *loco*,' I replied.

From that day forward Manolito used to go and visit her every evening and sit with the women who were praying to her for everlasting beauty. Like them he kissed her feet and arranged flowers in her hair, and he would linger on after they had gone, until I would have to come and fetch him away to eat his supper. I would find him sitting before her in the sunset, the red gold of the sky lending the glow of life to the woman's face, and often I would sit awhile and fall with him under the enchantment of that celestial face.

I will describe to you shortly the impression made by that face, but firstly I must tell you why she was so special to Manolito.

I cannot remember a time when he had not held in his mind the image of the lady to which he always referred as 'my woman'. It must have started when he was about twelve years old. We shared a bed in those days, and we would lie there before going to sleep, listening to the crickets and the owls, and the coughing of the jaguar, and often he would talk about 'my woman', describing her to me. He told me how she walked with him after he was asleep, holding his hand, teasing him, playfighting with him in the fields, kissing him on the cheek before he woke up or went on to another dream. For him, 'my woman' took on a reality so powerful that he never took a great interest in any other, not even in Raimunda, who could not get him to marry her even though she went to bed with him and got pregnant on purpose. Naturally I laughed at him and called him a dreamer, but he was sincere in his belief, and one day he told me that he had made love with 'my woman' for the first time, and that it had been the most beautiful experience imaginable. 'I promised to love her faithfully for ever,' he told me. 'From now on there will be no one else.' Naturally, I said that I had heard nothing and seen nothing during the night, and he showed me a bite on his arm that he claimed she had put there in sport. I said, 'You bit yourself, brother,' and he went to great lengths to prove to me that the imprint in his arm was beyond the reach of his mouth, and anyway the imprint was different from that made by his own teeth. In the end I gave in, just to keep him quiet.

But on subsequent nights I was awoken by him heaving and gasping beside me, moaning endearments, quivering with passion, and generally doing all those things on his own that my parents always did together when they thought that we were not around. It was at that time that I took to slinging a hammock outside under the silk-cotton tree, just to get a night's rest, and it was from that time that people began to notice his perpetual expression of sublime contentment and refer to him as 'the angel'. As for myself, I doubted his sanity, but I was his brother, and so I accepted him as he was, as a brother should, and I even envied him his nights of ecstasy, since I had never had any such myself, even with a phantom.

Manolito only had to see the corpse once to know that he had not waited and loved in vain. The materiality of 'my woman' seemed to him to vindicate what he had always known but had never been, able to prove even to himself.

But you should not get the wrong idea and start thinking that he transferred his sexual attentions to a dead body, because that is not what happened at all. He visited the body because it had once been the habitation of 'my woman'; he visited it because it made solid the stuff of dreams, as though the dream in itself was too ephemeral, too filmy, too evanescent to take hold of when he was not dreaming it. And at night his passion increased until the whole neighbourhood was awakened by the cries of his blissful consummations, and people began to protest to my parents about the ferocious animal noises, so that my brother had to move out and build himself a hut on the edge of the cemetery.

Perhaps you will understand my brother's obsession when I tell you that it was indeed a very perfect corpse. The eyes were closed, but Manolito knew that the eyes were violet. There was a perfection of symmetry in those features. The long black hair, parted in the middle, flowed down either side of her cheeks, reminding me of the way that a stream flows when seen from a high mountain, in the gentle curves of nature. The fact that her eyes were closed accentuated her appearance of preternatural peace and tranquillity, of the utmost repose, as though she were alive and in contemplation of something supremely happy. Her eyebrows had obviously never been plucked in vanity, and yet they arched like rainbows that spring from the nothingness of the empty sky. At the upper tip they tapered so finely that one could not say precisely where they finished, and at the bridge of the nose they were full and dark, reminding me of the silky fur of a fine black cat.

Her nose was straight, with the skin stretched so finely upon it that it had the quality that one perceives when looking through the body of a candle held up against a bright light. Her cheeks were a little shrunken in death, which served to

11

lend an extra curve to the formation of her cheekbones. Manolito told me that in reality her cheeks are quite full and that you cannot discern the line of the cheekbones at all, but in her tomb it gave her the appearance of noble blood and gentle education.

Perhaps it was her mouth that made a prisoner of my brother. It was the mouth of an innocent, and yet of one who knew all the carnality of a sensual woman in the prime of desire. The lips were closed, and yet they seemed to be at the point of opening, as though tempting one to a kiss. There was amusement playing about those lips, betrayed by the two tiny laughing lines at either end. It was the kind of amusement of one who knows a harmless secret; it made one want to say, OK, what's up? What are you hiding behind your back? Is it a present, or are you going to put a spider down my shirt when you think I am not looking?' It was a very sweet smile.

Because of that ineffable face I can remember next to nothing about the rest of the corpse. The face had a way of fixing your gaze in the expectation of being able to discern some subtle change of mood or the passing of a thought. I think that she had a ring with a large lilac stone on one hand, and I remember that the line of her body seemed as graceful and liquid as the flow of her hair upon her shoulders. All I can say is that she was so lovable that not only I, but also everyone in the village, thought of Manolito's passion as understandable.

But if you want to see her now you will be disappointed. She lives only in the memory of those who are now old, such as myself, because the fact is that the mountain swallowed her up.

We all believed that the mountain was dead, and in fact it was during the generation of my great-great-grandfather that the people stopped giving gifts to the mountain in order to calm its irascibility. It seemed that it was a god who had no longer any appetite for sacrifice or for activity, and even when it finally came back to life it did it with such gentleness that none of us felt terror or fell upon our knees to plead with the illogical Christian God or with the *orishas*. Of course Don

José was rushing about in a frenzy. He was shouting, 'Behold, I am against thee, O destroying mountain, saith the Lord, which destroyest all the earth; and I will stretch out my hand upon thee, and roll thee down from the rocks, and will make thee a burnt mountain. And they shall not take of thee a stone for a corner, nor a stone for foundations, but thou shalt be desolate for ever . . .' Don José was very pleased that the cemetery was being consumed, because he disapproved of the intercession of Don Salvador and Nuestra Señora de la Hermosura. In fact he once wrote in paint on Our Lady's tomb, 'Mystery, Babylon the Great, The Mother of Harlots and Abominations of the Earth'. Don José disapproved of female beauty, and he knew all the most depressing bits of the Bible by heart. But the rest of us just stood and watched from a safe distance, without any sense of mortal danger, until suddenly I remembered Manolito. The lava was flowing not down towards the village, but down towards the cemetery.

I confess that I did not run and arrive half dead with breathlessness and apprehension. I strolled over, knowing that Manolito had more sense than to lie in his hammock with molten rock lapping at the doorposts. I went just to check that he had made good his escape, and found him watching the spectacle safely to one side and fanning his face with his sombrero. 'Ay, brother,' he said. 'It is all going to one side, and our dead are safe. It is quite something, is it not?'

Unfortunately at that moment there was a kind of belching and gulping noise, and a new fissure opened in the rocks above the cemetery. With consternation in our faces we watched the magma squeeze like dung out of its imprisonment, curving and solidifying, hissing and steaming, and we both had the same thought.

'I will rescue Don Salvador,' I said, 'and you must rescue Nuestra Señora.' I ran to the tomb and slid the stone away in a desperate burst of strength, and I carried the saint away in my arms with time to spare even to go back and fetch one of the hands that had dropped off and the lower half of the left leg as well. I was very pleased and was congratulating myself when I saw that Manolito was still struggling with the slab of the tomb of his beloved. I was about to rush and help him when I saw that I could never make it there before I was consumed in the advancing furnace of golden flame. All I could do was shout above the rumbling of the entrails of the earth, and watch my brother perish.

Manolito did not run. The slab gave way at last, and I saw him size up his chances at the last second. He did what I would have done under the circumstances; he stepped inside the tomb and drew the slab after him, hoping that the lava would pass him by and that he would be protected by the stone sepulchre. If he cried out, I could not hear it above the groans and cracks of the rocks.

I have often thought about the poetic manner of his death. He died in the arms of the woman he had always loved, attempting to save her. He died before age had diminished him, and he died in a fire as incandescent and overwhelming as his own passion. If he had cried out in that inferno I would like to imagine that it would have been the same kind of cry that he used to make at night in the embrace of his woman.

We made him a saint, we have many songs about him now, and around here we refer to a lover as a 'manolito' or a manolita' , much as in Costa Rica they refer to youngsters as 'romanticos'. I go often to show the young people the place where my brother and his beloved embrace so deep beneath the rock, and I never fail to say that if they want to know the way that her hair fell down about her face, they have only to look at the beautiful curves that the lava made as it flowed and set above the cemetery where our ancestors slept.

Louis de Bernières is the author
of several novels, including
*Captain Corelli's Mandolin*,
published by Vintage.

# Rose Tremain

## THE CANDLE MAKER

FOR TWENTY-SEVEN YEARS, Mercedes Dubois worked in a laundry.

The laundry stood on a west-facing precipice in the hilltop town of Leclos. It was one of the few laundries in Corsica with a view of the sea.

On fine evenings, ironing at sunset was a pleasant – almost marvellous – occupation and for twenty-seven years Mercedes Dubois considered herself fortunate in her work. To her sister, Honorine, who made paper flowers, she remarked many times over the years: 'In my work, at least, I'm a fortunate woman. And Honorine, twisting wire, holding petals in her mouth, always muttered: 'I don't know why you have to put it like that.'

Then the laundry burned down.

The stone walls didn't burn, but everything inside them turned to black iron and black oil and ash. The cause was electrical, so the firemen said. Electricians in Leclos, they said, didn't know how to earth things properly.

The burning down of the laundry was the second tragedy in the life of Mercedes Dubois. She didn't know how to cope with it. She sat in her basement apartment and stared at her furniture. It was a cold December and Mercedes was wearing her old red anorak. She sat with her hands in her anorak pockets, wondering what she could do. She knew that in Leclos, once a thing was lost, it never returned. There had been a bicycle shop once, and a library and a lacemaker's. There had been fifty children and three teachers at the school; now, there were twenty children and one teacher. Mercedes pitied the lonely

15

teacher, just as she pitied the mothers and fathers of all the schoolchildren who had grown up and gone away. But there was nothing to be done about any of it. Certainly nothing one woman, single all her life, could do. Better not to remember the variety there had been. And better, now, not to remember the sunset ironing or the camaraderie of the mornings, making coffee, folding sheets. Mercedes Dubois knew that the laundry would never reopen because it had never been insured. Sitting with her hands in her anorak pockets, staring at her sideboard, was all there was to be done about it.

But after a while she stood up. She went over to the sideboard and poured herself a glass of anisette. She put it on the small table where she ate her meals and sat down again and looked at it. She thought: I can drink the damned anisette. I can do that at least.

She had always considered her surname right for her. She was as hard as wood. Wood, not stone. She could be pliant. And once, long ago, a set of initials had been carved on her heart of wood. It was after the carving of these initials that she understood how wrong for her her first name was. She had been christened after a Spanish saint, Maria de las Mercedes – Mary of the Mercies – but she had been unable to show mercy. On the contrary, what had consumed her was despair and malevolence. She had lain in her iron bed and consoled herself with thoughts of murder.

Mercedes Dubois: stoical but without forgiveness; a woman who once planned to drown her lover and his new bride and instead took a job in a laundry; what could she do, now that the laundry was gone?

Of her sister, Honorine, she asked the question: 'What can anyone do in so terrible a world?'

And Honorine replied: 'I've been wondering about that, because, look at my hands. I've got the beginnings of arthritis, see? I'm losing my touch with the paper flowers.'

'There you are,' said Mercedes. 'I don't know what anyone can do except drink.'

But Honorine, who was married to a sensible man, a

plasterer, shook a swollen finger at her sister and warned: 'Don't go down that road. There's always something. That's what we've been taught to believe. Why don't you go and sit in the church and think about it?'

'Have *you* gone and sat in the church and thought about it?' asked Mercedes.

'Yes.'

'And?'

'I noticed all the flowers in there are plastic these days. It's more durable than paper. We're going to save up and buy the kind of machinery you need to make a plastic flower.'

Mercedes left Honorine and walked down the dark, steep street, going towards home and the anisette bottle. She was fifty-four years old. The arrival of this second catastrophe in her life had brought back her memories of the first one.

The following day, obedient to Honorine, she went into the Church of St Vida, patron saint of lemon growers, and walked all around it very slowly, wondering where best to sit and think about her life. Nowhere seemed best. To Mercedes the child, this church had smelled of satin; now it smelled of dry rot. Nobody cared for it. Like the laundry, it wasn't insured against calamity. And the stench of calamity was here. St Vida's chipped plaster nostrils could detect it. She stood in her niche, holding a lemon branch to her breast, staring pitifully down at her broken foot. Mercedes thought: poor Vida, what a wreck, and no lemon growers left in Leclos. What can either Vida or I do in so desolate a world?

She sat in a creaking pew. She shivered. She felt a simple longing, now, for something to warm her while she thought about her life. So she went to where the votive candles flickered on their iron sconces – fourteen of them on the little unsteady rack – and warmed her hands there.

There was only one space left for a new candle and Mercedes thought: this is what the people of Leclos do in answer to loss: they come to St Vida's and light a candle. When the children leave, when the bicycle shop folds, when the last lacemaker dies, they illuminate a little funnel of air. It costs a franc. Even Honorine, saving up for her plastics machine, can afford one franc. And the candle is so much more than itself. The candle is the voice of a lover, the candle is a catch of mackerel, the candle is a drench of rain, a garden of marrows, a neon sign, a year of breath . . .

So Mercedes paid a franc and took a new candle and lit it and put it in the last vacant space on the rack. She admired it possessively: its soft colour, its resemblance to something living. But what *is* it? she asked herself. What *is* my candle? If only it could be something as simple as rain!

At this moment, the door of St Vida's opened and Mercedes heard footsteps go along the nave. She turned and recognised Madame Picaud, proprietor of the lost laundry. This woman had once been a café singer in Montparnasse. She'd worn feathers in her hair. On the long laundry afternoons, she used to sing ballads about homesickness and the darkness of bars. Now, she'd lost her second livelihood and her head was draped in a shawl.

Madame Picaud stood by the alcove of St Vida, looking up at the lemon branch and the saint's broken foot. Mercedes was about to slip away and leave the silence of the church to her former employer, when she had a thought that caused her sudden and unexpected distress: suppose poor Madame Picaud came, after saying a prayer to Vida, to light a candle and found that there was no space for it in the rack? Suppose Madame Picaud's candle was a laundry rebuilt and re-equipped with new bright windows looking out at the sea? Suppose the future of Madame Picaud – with which her own future would undoubtedly be tied – rested upon the ability of this single tongue of yellow fire to burn unhindered in the calamitous air of the Church of St Vida? And then it could not burn. It could not burn because there were too many other futures already up there flickering away on the rack.

Mercedes looked at her own candle and then at all the others. Of the fifteen, she judged that five or six had been burning for some time. And so she arrived at a decision about these: they were past futures. They had had their turn. What counted was the moment of lighting, or, if not merely the moment of lighting, then the moment of lighting and the first moments of burning. When the candles got stubby and started to burn unevenly, dripping wax into the tray, they were no longer love letters or olive harvests or cures for baldness or machines that manufactured flowers; they were simply old candles. They had to make way. No one had understood this until now. *I* understand it, said Mercedes to herself, because I know what human longing there is in Leclos. I know it because I am part of it.

She walked round to the back of the rack. She removed the seven shortest candles and blew them out. She rearranged the longer candles, including her own, until the seven spaces were all at the front, inviting seven new futures, one of which would be Madame Picaud's.

Then Mercedes walked home with the candles stuffed into the pockets of her red anorak. She laid them out on her table and looked at them.

She had never been petty or underhand.

She went to see the Curé the following morning and told him straight out that she wanted to be allowed to keep the future burning in Leclos by recycling the votive candles. She said: 'With the money you save, you could restore St Vida's foot.'

The Curé offered Mercedes a glass of wine. He had a fretful smile. He said: 'I've heard it's done elsewhere, in the great cathedrals, where they get a lot of tourists, but it's never seemed necessary in Leclos.'

Mercedes sipped her wine. She said: 'It's *more* necessary here than in Paris or Reims, because hope stays alive much longer in those places. In Leclos, everything vanishes. Everything.'

The Curé looked at her kindly. 'I was very sorry to hear about the laundry,' he said. 'What work will you do now?'

'I'm going to do this,' said Mercedes. 'I'm going to do the candles.'

He nodded. 'Fire, in Corsica, has always been an enemy. But I expect Madame Picaud had insurance against it?'

'No she didn't,' said Mercedes, 'only the free kind: faith and prayer.'

The Curé finished his glass of wine. He shook his head discreetly, as if he were a bidder at an auction who has decided to cease bidding.

'I expect you know,' he said after a moment, 'that the candles have to be of a uniform size and length?'

'Oh, yes.'

'And I should add that if there *are* savings of any import . . . then . . .'

'I don't wan't a few francs, Monsieur le Curé. I'm not interested in that. I just want to make more room for something to happen here, that's all.'

Collecting the candles and melting them down began to absorb her. She put away the anisette bottle. She went into the church at all hours. She was greedy for the candles. So she began removing even those that had burned for only a short time. She justified this to herself by deciding, once and for ever, that what mattered in every individual wish or intention was the act of lighting the candle – the moment of illumination. This alone. Nothing else. And she watched what people did. They lit their candles and looked at them for no more than a minute. Then they left. They didn't keep on returning to make sure their candles were still alight. 'The point is,' Mercedes explained to Honorine, 'they continue to burn in the imagination and the value you could set on the imagination would be higher than one franc. So the actual life of the candle is of no importance.'

'How can you be sure?' asked Honorine.

'I am sure. You don't need to be a philosopher to see it.'

'And what if a person did come back to check her individual candle?'

'The candles are identical, Honorine. A field of basil is indistinguishable from an offer of marriage.'

She had ordered six moulds from the forge and sent off for a hundred metres of cotton wick from a maker of night-lights in Ajaccio. The smell of bubbling wax pervaded her apartment. It resembled the smell of new leather, pleasant yet suffocating.

She began to recover from her loss of the job at the laundry. Because, in away, she thought, I've *become* a laundry; I remove the soiled hopes of the town and make them new and return them neatly to the wooden candle drawer.

The Social Security Office paid her a little sum of money each week. She wasn't really poor, not as poor as she'd feared, because her needs were few.

Sometimes, she walked out to the coast road and looked at the black remains of what had been spin-dryers and cauldrons of bleach, and then out beyond this pile of devastation to the sea, with its faithful mirroring of the sky and its indifference. She began to smell the spring on the salt winds.

News, in Leclos, travelled like fire. It leapt from threshold to balcony, from shutter to shutter.

One morning, it came down to Mercedes' door: 'Someone has returned, Mercedes. You can guess who.'

Mercedes stood in her doorway, blinking into the February sun. The bringer of the news was Honorine. Honorine turned and went away up the street leaving Mercedes standing there. The news burned in her throat. She said his name: Louis Cabrini.

She had believed he would never return to Leclos. He'd told her twenty-seven years ago that he'd grown to dislike the town, dislike the hill it sat on, dislike its name and its closed-in streets. He said. 'I've fallen in love, Mercedes – with a girl and with a place. I'm going to become a Parisian now.'

He had married his girl. She was a ballerina. Her name was Sylvie. It was by her supple, beautiful feet that the mind of Mercedes Dubois chained her to the ocean bed. For all that had been left her after Louis went away were her dreams of murder. Because she'd known, from the age of eighteen, that she, Mercedes, was going to be his wife. She had known and all of Leclos had known: Louis Cabrini and Mercedes Dubois were meant for each other. There would be a big wedding at the Church of St Vida and, after that, a future . . .

Then he went to Paris, to train as an engineer. He met a troupe of dancers in a bar. He came back to Leclos just the one time, to collect his belongings and say goodbye to Mercedes. He had stood with her in the square and it had been a sunny February day – a day just like this one, on which Honorine had brought news of his return – and after he'd finished speaking, Mercedes walked away without a word. She took twelve steps and then she turned round. Louis was standing quite still, watching her. He had taken her future away and this was all he could do – stand still and stare. She said: 'I'm going to kill you, Louis. You and your bride.'

Mercedes went down into her apartment. A neat stack of thirty candles was piled up on her table, ready to be returned to St Vida's. A mirror hung above the sideboard and Mercedes walked over to it and looked at herself. She had her father's square face, his deep-set brown eyes, his wiry hair. And his name. She would stand firm in the face of Honorine's news. She would go about her daily business in Leclos as if Louis were not there. If she chanced to meet him, she would pretend she hadn't recognised him. He was older than she was. He might by now, with his indulgent Parisian life, look like an old man. His walk would be slow.

But then a new thought came: suppose he hadn't returned to Leclos alone, as she'd assumed? Suppose when she went to buy her morning loaf she had to meet the fading beauty of the ballerina? And hear her addressed as Madame Cabrini? And see her slim feet in expensive shoes?

Mercedes put on her red anorak and walked up to Honorine's house. Honorine's husband, Jacques the plasterer, was there and the two of them were eating their midday soup in contented silence.

'You didn't tell me,' said Mercedes, 'has he come back alone?'

'Have some soup, said Jacques, 'you look pale.'

'I'm not hungry,' said Mercedes. 'I need to know, Honorine.'

'All I've heard is rumour,' said Honorine.

'Well?'

'They say she left him. Some while back. They say he's been in poor health ever since.'

Mercedes nodded. Not really noticing what she did, she sat down at Honorine's kitchen table. Honorine and Jacques put down their spoons and looked at her. Her face was waxy.

Jacques said: 'Give her some soup, Honorine.' Then he said: 'There's too much history in Corsica. It's in the stone.'

When Mercedes left Honorine's she went straight to the church. On the way, she kept her head down and just watched her shadow moving along ahead of her as, behind her, the sun went down.

There was nobody in St Vida's. Mercedes went straight to the candle sconces. She snatched up two low-burning candles and blew them out. She stood still a moment, hesitating. Then she blew out all the remaining candles. It's wretched, wretched, she thought: all this interminable, flickering, optimistic light; wretched beyond comprehension.

After February, in Corsica, the spring comes fast. The *maquis* starts to bloom. The mimosas come into flower.

Mercedes was susceptible to the perfume of things. So much so that, this year, she didn't want even to *see* the mimosa blossom. She wanted everything to stay walled up in its own particular winter. She wanted clouds to gather and envelop the town in a dark mist.

She crept about the place like a thief. She had no conversations. She scuttled here and there, not looking, not noticing. In her apartment, she kept the shutters closed. She worked on the candles by the light of a single bulb.

Honorine came down to see her. 'You can't go on like this, Mercedes,' she said. 'You can't live this way.'

'Yes, I can,' said Mercedes.

'He looks old,' said Honorine, 'his skin's yellowy. He's not the handsome person he used to be.'

Mercedes said nothing. She thought, no one in this place, not even my sister, has ever understood what I feel.

'You ought to go and meet him,' said Honorine. 'Have a drink with him. It's time you forgave him.'

Mercedes busied herself with the wax she was melting in a saucepan. She turned her back towards Honorine.

'Did you hear what I said?' asked Honorine.

'Yes,' said Mercedes, 'I heard.'

After Honorine had left, Mercedes started to weep. Her tears fell into the wax and made it spit. Her cheeks were pricked with small burns. She picked up a kitchen cloth and buried her head in it. She thought, what no one understands is that this darkness isn't new. I've been in it in my mind for twenty-seven years, ever since that February morning in the square when the mimosas were coming into flower. There were moments when it lifted – when those big sunsets came in at the laundry window, for instance – but it always returned, as night follows day; always and always.

And then she thought, but Honorine is right, it is intolerable. I should have done what I dreamed of doing. I should have killed him. Why was I so cowardly? I should have cut off his future – all those days and months of his happy life in Paris that I kept seeing like a film in my head: the ballerina's hair falling on his body; her feet touching his feet under the dainty patisserie table; their two summer shadows moving over the water of the Seine. I should have ended it as I planned, and then I would have been free of him and out of the darkness and I could have had a proper life.

And now. She was in Leclos, in her own town that she'd never left, afraid to move from her flat, gliding to and from the church like a ghost, avoiding every face, sunk into a loneliness so deep and fast it resembled the grave. Was this how the remainder of her life was to be spent?

She prised the buttons of wax from her cheeks with her fingernails. She took the saucepan off the gas flame and laid it aside, without pouring its contents into the candle moulds. It was a round-bottomed pan and Mercedes could imagine the smooth, rounded shape into which the wax would set.

She ran cold water on to her face, drenching her hair, letting icy channels of water eddy down her neck and touch her breasts. Her mind had recovered from its futile weeping

24

and had formulated a plan and she wanted to feel the chill of the plan somewhere near her heart.

She lay awake all night. She had decided at last to kill Louis Cabrini.

Not with her own hands, face to face. Not like that.

She would do it slowly. From a distance. With all the power of the misery she'd held inside her for twenty-seven years.

Morning came and she hadn't slept. She stared at the meagre strips of light coming through the shutters. In this basement apartment, it was impossible to gauge what kind of day waited above. But she knew that what waited above, today, was the plan. It was a Friday. In Mercedes' mind, the days of the week were different colours. Wednesday was red. Friday was a pallid kind of yellow.

She dressed and put on her apron. She sat at her kitchen table drinking coffee and eating bread. She heard two women go past her window, laughing. She thought: that was the other beautiful thing that happened in the laundry – laughter.

When the women had walked on by and all sound of them had drained away, Mercedes said aloud: 'Now.'

She cleared away the bread and coffee. She lit one ring of the stove and held above it the saucepan full of wax, turning it like a chef turns an omelette pan, so that the flames spread an even heat round the body of the wax. She felt it come loose from the saucepan, a solid lump. 'Good,' she said.

She set out a pastry board on the table. She touched its smooth wooden surface with her hand. Louis Cabrini had been childishly fond of pastries and cakes. In her mother's kitchen, Mercedes used to make him *tarte tatin* and *apfelstrudel*.

She turned out the lump of wax on to the pastry board. It was yellowy in colour. The more she recycled the candles the yellower they became.

Now she had a round dome of wax on which to begin work.

She went to the bookcase, which was almost empty except for a green, chewed set of the collected works of Victor Hugo and an orange edition of *Lettres de mon moulin* by Alphonse Daudet. Next to Daudet was a book Mercedes had borrowed from the library twenty-seven years ago to teach herself about sex and had never returned, knowing perhaps that the library, never very efficient with its reminders, would close in due time. It was called *Simple Anatomy of the Human Body*. It contained drawings of all the major internal organs. On page fifty-nine was a picture of the male body unclothed, at which Mercedes used to stare.

Mercedes put the book next to the pastry board, under the single light. She turned the pages until she found the drawing of the heart. The accompanying text read: 'The human heart is small, relative to its importance. It is made up of four chambers, the right and left auricle and the right and left ventricle . . .'

'All right,' said Mercedes.

Using the drawing as a guide, she began to sculpt a heart out of the wax dome. She worked with a thin filleting knife and two knitting needles of different gauges.

Her first thought as she started the sculpture was: the thing it most resembles is a fennel root and the smell of fennel resembles in its turn the smell of anisette.

The work absorbed her. She didn't feel tired any more. She proceeded carefully and delicately, striving for verisimilitude. She knew that this heart was larger than a heart is supposed to be and she thought, well, in Louis Cabrini's case, it swelled with pride – pride in his beautiful wife, pride in his successful career, pride in being a Parisian, at owning a second-floor apartment, at eating in good restaurants, at buying roses at dusk to take home to his woman. Pride in leaving Leclos behind. Pride in his ability to forget the past.

She imagined his rib-cage expanding to accommodate this swollen heart of his.

Now and again, she made errors. The she had to light a match and pass it over the wax to melt it – to fill too deep an abrasion or smooth too jagged an edge. And she noticed in time that this slight re-melting of the heart gave it a more liquid, living appearance. This was very satisfactory. She began to relish it. She would strike a match and watch an ooze begin, then blow it out and slowly repair the damage she'd caused.

It was becoming, just as she'd planned, her plaything. Except that she'd found more ways to wound it than she'd imagined. She had thought that, in the days to come, she would pierce it or cut it with something – scissors, knives, razor blades. But now she remembered that its very substance was unstable. She could make it bleed. She could make it disintegrate. It could empty itself out. And then, if she chose, she could rebuild it, make it whole again. She felt excited and hot. She thought: I have never had power over anything; this has been one of the uncontrovertible facts of my life.

As the day passed and darkness filled the cracks in the shutters, Mercedes began to feel tired. She moved the anatomy book aside and laid her head on the table beside the pastry board. She put her hand inside her grey shirt and squeezed and massaged her nipple, and her head filled with dreams of herself as a girl, standing in the square, smelling the sea and smelling the mimosa blossom, and she fell asleep.

She thought someone was playing a drum. She thought there was a march coming up the street.

But it was a knocking on her door.

She raised her head from the table. Her cheek was burning hot from lying directly under the light bulb. She had no idea whether it was night-time yet. She remembered the heart, almost finished, in front of her. She thought the knocking on her door could be Honorine coming to talk to her again and tell her she couldn't go on living the way she was.

She didn't want Honorine to see the heart. She got up and draped a clean tea towel over it, as though it were a newly baked cake. All around the pastry board were crumbs of wax and used matches. Mercedes tried to sweep them into her hand and throw them in the sink. She felt dizzy after her sleep on the table. She staggered about like a drunk. She knew she'd been having beautiful dreams.

When she opened her door, she saw a man standing there. He wore a beige mackintosh and a yellow scarf. Underneath the mackintosh, his body looked bulky. He wore round glasses. He said: 'Mercedes?'

She put a hand up to her red burning cheek. She blinked at him. She moved to close the door in his face, but he anticipated this and put out a hand, trying to keep the door open.

'Don't do that,' he said. 'That's the easy thing to do.'

'Go away,' said Mercedes.

'Yes. OK. I will, I promise. But first let me in. Please. Just for ten minutes.'

Mercedes thought: if I didn't feel so dizzy, I'd be stronger. I'd be able to push him out. But all she did was hold on to the door and stare at him. Louis Cabrini. Wearing glasses. His curly hair getting sparse. His belly fat.

He came into her kitchen. The book of human anatomy was still open on the table, next to the covered heart.

He looked all around the small, badly lit room. From his mackintosh pocket, he took out a bottle of red wine and held it out to her. 'I thought we could drink some of this.'

Mercedes didn't take the bottle. 'I don't want you here,' she said. 'Why did you come back to Leclos?'

'To die,' he said. 'Now, come on. Drink a glass of wine with me. One glass.'

She turned away from him. She fetched two glasses and put them on the table. She closed the anatomy book.

'Corkscrew?' he asked.

She went to her dresser drawer and took it out. It was an old-fashioned thing. She hardly ever drank wine any more, except at Honorine's. Louis put the wine on the table. 'May I take my coat off?' he said.

Under the smart mackintosh, he was wearing comfortable clothes, baggy brown trousers, a black sweater. Mercedes laid the mackintosh and the yellow scarf over the back of a chair. 'You don't look as if you're dying,' she said, 'you've got quite fat.'

He laughed. Mercedes remembered this laugh by her side in her father's little vegetable garden. She had been hoeing onions. Louis had laughed and laughed at something she'd said about the onions.

'I'm being melodramatic,' he said. 'I'm not going to die tomorrow. I mean that my life in Paris is over. I'm in Leclos now till I peg out! I mean that this is all I've got left to do. The rest is finished.'

'Everything finishes,' said Mercedes.

'Well,' said Louis, 'I wouldn't say that. Leclos is just the same, here on its hill. Still the same cobbles and smelly gutters. Still the same view of the sea.'

'You're wrong,' said Mercedes, 'nothing lasts here in Leclos. Everything folds or moves away.'

'But not the place itself. Or you. And here we both are. Still alive.'

'If you can call it living.'

'Yes, it's living. And you've baked a cake, I see. Baking is being alive. Now here. Have a sip of wine. Let me drink a toast to *you*.'

She needed the wine to calm her, to get her brain thinking properly again. So she drank. She recognised at once that Louis had brought her expensive wine. She offered him a chair and they both sat down at the table. Under the harsh light, Mercedes could see that Louis' face looked creased and sallow.

'Honorine told me you'd been hiding from me.'

'I don't want you here in Leclos.'

'That saddens me. But perhaps you'll change your mind in time?'

'No. Why should I?'

'Because you'll get used to my being here. I'll become part of the place, like furniture, or like poor old Vida up at the church with her broken foot.'

'You've been in the church? I've never seen you in there.'

'Of course I've been in. It was partly the church that brought me back. I've been selfish with my money for most of my life, but I thought if I came back to Leclos I would start a fund to repair that poor old church.'

'The church doesn't need you.'

'Well, it needs someone. You can smell the damp in the stone . . .'

'It needs *me*! I'm the one who's instituted the idea of economy. No one thought of it before. They simply let everything go to waste. *I'm* the one who understood about the candles. It didn't take a philosopher. It's simple once you see it.'

'What's simple?'

'I can't go into it now. Not to you. It's simple and yet not. And with you I was never good at explaining things.'

'Try,' said Louis.

'No,' said Mercedes.

They were silent. Mercedes drank her wine. She thought, this is the most beautiful wine I've ever tasted. She wanted to pour herself another glass, but she resisted.

'I'd like you to leave now,' she said.

Louis smiled. Only in his smile and in his laughter did Mercedes recognise the young man whose wife she should have been. 'I've only just arrived, Mercedes, and there's so much we could talk about . . .'

'There's nothing to talk about.'

The smile vanished. 'Show me some kindness,' he said. 'I haven't had the happy life you perhaps imagined. I made a little money, that's all. That's all I have to show. The only future I can contemplate is here, so I was hoping—'

'Don't stay in Leclos. Go somewhere else. Anywhere . . .'

'I heard about the fire.'

'What?'

'The fire at the laundry. But I think it's going to be all right.'

'Of course it's not going to be all right. You don't understand how life is in Leclos any more. You just walk back and walk in, when no one invited you . . .'

'The church "invited" me. But also Madame Picaud. She wrote and asked me what could be done when the laundry burned down. I told her I would try to help.'

'There's no insurance.'

'No.'

'How can you help, then?'

'I told you, all I have left is a little money. One of my investments will be a new laundry.'

Mercedes said nothing. After a while, Louis stood up. 'I'll go now, he said, 'but three things brought me back, you know. St Vida, the laundry and you. I want your forgiveness. I would like us to be friends.'

'I can't forgive you,' said Mercedes. 'I never will.'

'You may. In time. You may surprise yourself. Remember your name, Mercedes: Mary of the Mercies.'

Mercedes drank the rest of the wine.

She sat very still at her table, raising the glass to her lips and sipping and sipping until it was all gone. She found herself admiring her old sticks of furniture and the shadows in the room that moved as if to music.

She got unsteadily to her feet. She had no idea what time it could be. She heard a dog bark.

She got out her candle moulds and set them in a line. She cut some lengths of wick. Then she put Louis Cabrini's waxen heart into the rounded saucepan and melted it down and turned it back into votive candles.

Rose Tremain's latest book,
*The Way I Found Her*, is
published by Vintage.

# Brian Keenan

## EXTRACT FROM A NOVEL IN PROGRESS

*Turlough Carolan, the blind harpist, relates his
understanding of Light to his poet friend, Charles McCabe.
The narrator is McCabe's apprentice.*

'I CAN'T REMEMBER when you finished talking and I
started dreaming. But I dreamt I saw some people I knew
standing off the banks of your cursed river. I was in a boat but
I wasn't sure whether I was rowing towards or away from
them.'

McCabe laughed in return and said that he wasn't sure
himself when he finished talking but he remembered lighting
a candle and leaving it beside Turlough's bed. 'Are you really
afraid of the dark,' he asked. Carolan stood silent by the door,
then quietly answered with another question.

'Did I say that?'

'You did,' confirmed McCabe, 'but I thought you were
playing with me so I said nothing until you asked for the
candle . . . But it's a queer notion, now, as I think on it . . . A
blind man who's scared of the dark! What in hell's gates did
you mean.'

I was about to close my eyes and sleep for I had as little as
both of them and I hoped they might both go off somewhere
together but the conversation that followed was one that
taught me more than all my years with McCabe. I am not sure
I should have heard it, and probably would not have if the
drink had not made them both forgetful of my presence. I lay

and listened, afraid to move as Carolan spoke.

'I'm not sure I know. Maybe it was the drink in me . . . When I was young I loved the light. As a child it seemed to cast a spell over me. I would sit for hours at the open door and watch the light flowing over the surface of the land. I didn't really look for the sun. I looked for the light reflecting off everything. A rock, the wall of our house, how it glistened on our window and threw a long column of itself from the door into our kitchen. I stood in it. It was part of me. I thought it had come specially for me.'

McCabe took a seat by the fire and listened. He drew heavily on his pipe and studied the silhouette of his friend in the bright doorway. There was something about the way Carolan spoke. His voice was different somehow. I can't explain it, but it was almost as if he was someone else. It certainly wasn't the Turlough Carolan of the night before. For some reason I was afraid of what he said, it was so confusing!

'Even the night-time could not dispel my fascination with the light. Darkness was still light. But it was different. It was slower or something. It was only light in another form. In the dark I could dream, even with my eyes open.'

Carolan stopped and rubbed his eyes. Then he turned to McCabe and said brightly.

'You know, children know more than we think! When I was a child I knew everything with the whole of my being. But now I am old, I only know things with my head . . . Perhaps that's why I am afraid of the dark!'

I was now sure that Carolan was not talking from the effects of drink. The residue of the night's alcohol might have made this conversation easier but it was by no means the root cause of it, and it certainly wasn't the ramblings of a drunk.

'I'm going to let you into a secret, my friend. Being blind is not what you may imagine. People say that being blind means not to see . . . but they are wrong. The blind are only blind if they insist on seeing with their eyes . . . When I couldn't see things in the way I had before, I felt devastated and angry and anguish filled me with despair. And so for too long I lived without seeing . . .'

Turlough's tone of voice changed. It was urgent. He raised his index fingers and tapped on his temples beside his eyes.

'... But not because of blindness ... you see I was still looking with the eyes I no longer had ... No, no I mean I was looking the wrong way ... Then I met Fionnuala Quinn and she began to prise my eyes open ... I began to look more closely, not at things, but at the new world blindness had brought me ... it was like a radiance emanating from a place I hardly knew was there. Now I think I live too much in my head and I can't find that place. That's the problem with poets too, and that's what I was trying to explain to you last night.'

As he finished he turned from the door and walked towards the fire where he stood warming his hands. McCabe sat behind him in silence. With his back to him, Turlough asked,

'Does my secret confuse you?'

'It's queer talk all right!' McCabe simply.

'It took me a long time to understand these things. And I am not sure I do now. You see I was already a young man when I became blind. But as I learned to leave my sighted world behind and enter my own new world I began to feel indescribable relief and happiness. I was filled with confidence and gratitude as if a prayer had been answered. At first these moments came in short bursts, then they grew longer, slowly, light and joy came to me. They came as one sure thing in my experience.'

McCabe could not restrain the words. 'It's like a dream, an enchantment. It's like magic!'

'But it was not magic for me. It was reality, and my whole being was filled with it. It seemed as if I lived in a stream of light ... And here's what's stranger, McCabe, colours also survived. This inner light threw its colour on things and people. Everyone had a colour that I never saw before I was blind. It was as much a part of them as their face or their voice ... For a long time I did not understand all this; I only knew I was living it and in time I would understand it. But I couldn't speak to anyone about it. I became confused and angry, I frightened people I suppose.'

He moved away from the fire and asked McCabe to fill him

a pipe as he pulled a chair to the table.

'Does this begin to answer all your insane questions of last night?' he asked.

McCabe was, for a moment, perplexed. There had been much drunken debate and he was not sure what Carolan was referring to. He mumbled out his confusion as an excuse, but Carolan would not let him finish. His voice had lost is calmness.

'The dark, man, The dark. That passionate majestic dark that you believe makes great art . . . It's not in me . . .'

He took a long pause as if he wanted the statement to sink in, then he lowered his voice and whispered . . .

'Though as I get older I have premonitions of it, I feel shadows. Age leaves its shadows on us all.'

McCabe knew that at this moment Carolan was not feeling as self-assured as his words had suggested. He quickly finished fuelling and lit the pipe he held. Then he placed it into Carolan's hand saying,

'As for those shadows, you, my old friend, have less cause to fear them than the rest of us.'

For several long minutes the two of them sat in silence drawing on their pipes. I didn't know whether to pretend I had just woken up. I was thinking what excuse I could make to leave the cottage. The silence was suffocating.

Brian Keenan is the author of
*An Evil Cradling*,
published by Vintage.

# Seamus Deane

## CAROLE DREAMS OF THE WIZARD
### Extract from a Work in Progress

THERE IS SOMETHING strange in the air around me. Has been since I woke, hours ago. I hear, now and then, a far-off booming, as of artillery fire; I drift reluctantly in an undulating sleep, as though I was under water, enduring an ambient vagueness, wanting to be up above where there is a clean shore, where all the sounds are bright and leisurely, with people walking in parks and a church bell-tower pealing and tingling within the complacencies of a Sunday morning into homes where other people sit around in their dressing gowns and sip fragrant coffee amid mounds of newsprint and unlistened-to music that lies estranged in rooms without ears. I have a fear that I am slipping away beyond all this, from where my heart longs to be.

Last night I had a dream. A young man was speaking to me; he was bent over me and I could see his blue mouth opening and closing. It was a complicated mouth; it seemed intricate as a machine, as though it had more working parts than is usual. The roof of the mouth was especially blue and had a visible cellular structure that changed rapidly as he spoke. He did not love me, I knew that, but he was intent, he had such a way of moving his hands as he talked that he seemed to cut my body shape out of the bed and let everything around me fall way in black shavings. It was like the photographic negative of an embrace; I wanted to be resolved into myself again, but while he bent over me I was minussed. Not that I wanted him to embrace me; I wanted to embrace myself. But

I could not move. His sexual power was low, despite his good looks. It wasn't that that held me, it was his rapid speech that had all the articulations of speech movement, but there was no voice, just this sound as though a voice were being pulled out of a sheath but had not yet come right out, as though a weapon packed *in excelsior* were being withdrawn. But it was the sound of a voice that was beginning to arrive. That was the primary sensation – expectancy. Something was about to arrive, happen, and I was being lifted out of my bed, out of my room, out of my life towards it. Then, as I was raised close to him, his mouth went green and fanged, like a vicious and ancient animal's, salivating. I woke up in fright and smelled the dust in the carpet, heated as though the sun had been shining on it for hours. But it was still night. The fear brightened in me, as though I suddenly had had an idea. It did not paralyse me, it just made me alert. Something was going to happen.

I knew that. My body was a confusion of signals – itches, flash pains, micro-sweats, gas balling under my heart, the rims of my ears icy cold. Distress signals, as though all my minor forces were fleeing at the appearance within their domain of some minatory and emerging shape or creature. It was like – what can I say? – like an ancient castle coming out of the mists of a time into which it had disappeared, like a face looking for its features as a hand scrabbles for a grip on a glossy surface? What? What? It was something that would be formed, that had once been formed, was now formless and would be formed again, that was going to glitter with the lotions of newness but was as grey and solid as death.

Then I realised my thighs were wet, the bed was soaked. I had urinated in my sleep. What would the concierge say? Could I dry the sheets out before morning on the steam radiator? Would it be on? I was too lethargic to get up and see, to wash myself. I slept again and now, it is morning and the sheets are dry. I must have dreamed I wet the bed. But I don't think so.

When I got out this morning, the air was so clean, the streets were absorbed in a daffodil light, the child in my belly was heavy and gentle, suspended in her sac, the sky rose for miles and I knew I had to be afraid for he was near, that young man, sexless and beautiful, so near, although I could not see him or hear him. But with every other sense, touch and smell, I could feel him and knew he was snarling and smiling within this heavenly light that was such a blessing to me at that time, so cool and calming in its extraordinariness.

I had little money left. I spent the day walking, sitting on park benches, eating once, a long, slow lunch – a mushroom omelette, two cups of coffee. I watched a man close to me drink red wine, careful not to let him see me watch him. He had spilt a little on the metal table and it lay there in a blob, under his sleeve which time and again almost touched it, missed, time and again, until, yes, it touched and his pale cream linen sleeve snatched the red surface off the spill. I left before he saw what he had done. The tiny incident gratified me in an odd way; I had liked watching the wine finally make its appearance on his sleeve, after so many passes over its sleek surface. As I left the café, I smelt a dark tobacco smoke that caramelised in my nostrils and looked back over my shoulder, knowing he was there, knowing I would not see him, feeling him tempt me to want him, knowing he could not really be wanted physically despite his contrived appeals, knowing I already knew that. I swallowed the taste of the tobacco into my lungs and felt the child refrain within me and I went on.

Seamus Deane's novel,
*Reading in the Dark*, is
published by Vintage.

# Charles Handy

## A Taste of the Sublime

LIFE CAN BE A trudge, working to eat and eating to work –
for what? I need, we all need, the occasional reminder that the
world is an extraordinary place and that people are capable of
extraordinary things.

A poverty of aspiration – a hurtful but true criticism of
much of Britain after the war, and of many inner-city areas in
America today – can be fatal to a continuing exploration of
all the possibilities in life. Enough can mean full stop, rather
than a springboard for something new, unless imagination is
stirred, senses aroused, and ideas and questions kindled.
Nature at its best, animals in the wild, the starry skies above,
said Kant, that stern philosopher, but also man-made things
and occasions, the arts in all their forms, festivals and feasts,
acts of great generosity and courage, of love and sacrifice –
such things can all provide us with a glimpse of excellence and
a taste of the sublime. God, said Dame Julian of Norwich, is
in everything that is good, and God is in each one of us. If God
be another word for The Good, then to find the good in
ourselves we need first to look for it in the good things of the
world, not least to remind ourselves that there *is* good out
there, and therefore, most likely in ourselves. Sad must be
those who never see it.

St Petersburg in winter is a magnificent but uncomfortable
place. It is cold, grey, wet and gloomy, or can be in November
which is when I was last there. The Russian people whom I
met were likewise grey and gloomy. Capitalism has not had
the rejuvenating effect in St Petersburg that it has had in parts
of Eastern Europe, and perhaps in some other parts of Russia.

There is nothing much in the shops, and few have the wherewithal with which to buy what there is. If I were a St Petersburger in the winter I would be inclined to wonder what life was all about, and whether any of it was worth it.

Until, that is, I went to the Mariinsky Theatre to see the *Nutcracker Suite* ballet. This theatre is a magnificent place, a green and gold extravaganza – and packed with people. The most expensive tickets, for Russians, were less than £5 (still dear for them) but most were much less. Whole families were there, as, were school classes with their teachers, young and old alike, some smart, some shabby, all agog.

The ballet is unashamedly romantic, and the last act a fantasy of a ballet lover's heaven. Even the most cynical could not help but be stirred by its beauty, particularly when danced traditionally but to perfection by the Kirov School. I went out into the cold night wondering about the contradictions – the poverty and inefficiency outside and the sumptuous excellence inside. Was this the Russian version of bread and circuses, a way to pacify the mob, to make up for all their hardships, or do the Russians see the arts as a glimpse of the transcendent, something that will help us make sense of life, and therefore to be made available to all, as cheaply as possible?

Looking at the rapt faces of the audience that night and watching the crowds of ordinary Russians pouring into the Hermitage the next day, with its unbeatable collection of paintings, I am inclined to the more elevated view. These people weren't there just to get out of the cold, they were coming to see some things that were near to the sublime and the eternal. If they went away uplifted for a while, or pondering on the real meaning of life, of what endured and what was passing fancy, surely this was no bad thing. If the evening gave them the impulse to rise above their present condition, surely even better.

It will be interesting to see whether the Mariinsky Theatre and the Kirov Ballet survive when Russia eventually embraces the free market. Put art of this quality into the marketplace, with realistic costs and prices, and it inevitably becomes expensive, a playground for the rich. Too bad, then, if you are poor and can't get your own taste of truth and beauty from the great theatres, concert halls or museums. The market, one has to conclude, is not always the best guarantee of free choice or democracy.

Yet, paradoxically, for the market to work in the sectors where it does work well, we need to know that there is more to life than marketplace success. Those who struggle unsuccessfully in that marketplace will better tolerate the riches of the successful if they realise that there are some things that money cannot buy. The arts in their many different guises offer some hint of that other deeper world. Art, said Picasso, blows away the everyday cobwebs from the soul. All should have the chance to taste that breeze. Market economy or not, some things perhaps should not be priced too high, so that they are available to all.

In Italy, three years ago, the workers throughout Tuscany went on strike for a day – in protest at the bomb which destroyed a part of the Uffizi Gallery in Florence. It is hard to imagine the people of New York or London doing the same, but to the people of Tuscany their art is their heritage, it enriches their everyday life. They are fortunate – they see it all around them every day, in the architecture and sculptures of their cities, in the frescos which still embellish the walls of their churches. In summer, their towns are full of music. Most of it is there for free.

We speak, in most of America and Europe, of education and health care as the entitlements of every citizen in what we would like to think of as our civilized societies. In a truly civilized society, that entitlement would include open access to all the things that stir our imaginations. If we can't put those things in our streets, we should let the people through the doors. It would compensate a little for the inefficiencies that are inevitable in any free-enterprise system, and would permit more tolerance, encourage more creativity and release more talent. It might even turn out to be a good market investment for the nation.

Most of all, however, the arts put the rest of our life in

perspective. At peak moments they help to move us on, to make the struggle seem worthwhile. That happened for me one summer in Spoleto. Forty years ago, Gian Carlo Menotti, looking for a small town in which to stage a festival of music and theatre in his native Italy, settled on this beautiful but previously unnoticed place in Southern Umbria. Today, the three weeks of the Spoleto Festival attract distinguished musicians and performers from all over the world, and the little town hums with music and the arts under the summer sun. Conviviality is in the air. It is good to be alive, and to be there.

The climax is the final 'Concerto in Piazza', staged in front of the magnificent cathedral, with an audience of some 6,000 seated in the piazza and stretching way up the long flight of steps behind. That year they performed Mahler's *Resurrection Symphony*, all one and a half hours of it, complete with choir, and trumpeters on the balcony, on a balmy night, with Menotti, now 85, there to introduce it. Magic, of a sort, even if the gold-bedangled part of the audience had clearly come from Rome more to be seen than to listen. But there was, to this listener anyway, a message behind the magic.

Writing about this symphony, Mahler observed that each of us must, at some time, question what it is all for. Is life more than a scherzo, he asked, to be rattled through as quickly and harmoniously as possible? Or is there more to it? I will answer that question, he said, in the final movement. That movement is an exciting, upsetting and, at the same time, uplifting piece of music. I listened to it once, on my headphones, on a plane coming back to Britain over the Atlantic, as dawn was breaking above the clouds, when nature and the music seemed in complete harmony. It was even more powerful in Spoleto.

Each must make their own interpretation of what Mahler was trying to say in that last movement. For me, it was a declaration that, for all its ups and downs, life was about more than surviving – there could be something glorious about it, it could contribute to a better world. That leaves one with a personal challenge, to do something glorious with one's life. It is also, I believe, a challenge for every organization and every business that has, in effect, bought large chunks of other people's lives. It is not enough to offer a scherzo.

The Kirov Ballet and Mahler in Spoleto sound splendidly élitist. They happen to tingle my own imagination more than a pop concert. For each our own. For me, too, a good play in the theatre is a form of highlighter, emphasizing aspects of life which need to be thought about. Others find that different perspective in films or novels. Nor does one have to be rich or privileged to provide others with a hint of greater things, to make something glorious. Alan Bennett, the British playwright, recounts in one of his essays how as a young lad he used to go to the symphony concerts in Leeds and ride home on the tram afterwards along with several of the musicians 'who would sit there, rather shabby and ordinary, and often with tab ends in their mouths, worlds away from the Delius, Walton and Brahms they had been playing. It was a first lesson to me that . . . ordinary middle-aged men in raincoats can be instruments of the sublime.'

'Instruments of the Sublime.' Yes, indeed – ordinary people can always raise the world a notch or two for those around them, creating another sort of feel-good factor. And it doesn't have to be in concert halls – it can happen in our own families, where life can often mean just getting through the day, or at work, where work can be a boring four-letter word instead of the creative, exciting thing it's meant to be. And it doesn't need money. It's an attitude of mind. Elizabeth, in her work as a portrait photographer, unusually I think, sets out to make portraits that encourage people to feel good about themselves, to show what is best in them. It can change their lives. We can all do something to stimulate someone's imagination. It is, in fact, I believe, not only our privilege to be an instrument of the sublime, but our responsibility, and it's a lot more fun than looking at a bank statement and wondering if that is all there is to life.

Unless you believe in reincarnation, it is not given to us humans to see more than one life on this earth, but it is possible to leave some imprint of yourself behind, thus achieving a sort of immortality, although one to be enjoyed by others, not ourselves. We can add light to the lives of others after we have gone. It is an idea captured in that most poignant of military memorial inscriptions: 'For your to-morrow, we gave our today'. Leaving an imprint does not have to be this sacrificial, thank God. Gifts of ourselves take many forms, but they are all unique.

Maybe, I reflected in that piazza in Spoleto, Mahler was hinting that if we are to deserve some sort of immortality, even to contemplate the notion that we have left an indelible mark on time, then we have to aspire to be something special, to change and grow. We live on in others, thereby. For many, the children that they rear are their best legacy, their enduring gift to humanity. For others it is the work they do, or the businesses they create. For some it is the lives they saved or bettered, the kids they taught or the sick they healed. The sobering thought is that individuals and societies are not, in the end, remembered for how they made their money, but for how they spent it.

A headstone in the graveyard that records the millions made by the body buried there impresses none of the passers by. It is what was done with the millions that counts. The imprint we leave on the world is the only form of temporary immortality of which we can be sure. In the end, that is where we find our true identity. Anything else is only a step upon the ladder. A person who recognizes this will understand that 'enough' is an invitation to climb higher on the ladder, and a society which buys into the contribution ethic will use Capitalism as its tool and not its purpose.

Some contributions come early in life, some much later. We can take comfort from Degas, who painted his most en-chanting portraits after most people's normal retirement age. These works all came about because he felt a failure. When he hit 60, Degas looked back at his life and work and decided that it amounted to nothing. The vogue for his impressionist art seemed to have passed, and now it all seemed to him a flash in the pan, a waste of paint. He turned his back on life and retreated to his dark, brown studio, determined to create, at last, something special, not for anyone else to see or buy, just for himself. He died at 83, evicted from his studio, blind, lonely and depressed. Only now can we see, for the first time, the full, glorious fruits of his last twenty years.

You don't have to be 60 and a temperamental artist to look back at your life and wonder if it wasn't all chaff in the wind. From time to time I take out my old appointment diaries and wonder who all those people were that I was meeting, what those committees were all about, and what, if anything, we achieved. Nelson Mandela has seen *his* life's work fully justified, but he says in his autobiography that he wondered at times, during those dark prison years, whether he might not have done better to have been an ordinary lawyer, at home with his wife and family.

But it is not for us to judge our own life. Nor can we necessarily expect any judgement in our own lifetime. Degas would have been astounded to see the admiring crowds around his late-life pictures. His work inspires us, as does his example. Cathedrals also inspire. It is not only their grandeur or splendour, but the thought that they often took more than fifty years to build. Those who designed them, those who first worked on them, knew for certain that they would never see them finished. They knew only that they were creating something glorious which would stand for centuries, long after their own names had been forgotten. They had their own dream of the sublime and of immortality. We may not need any more cathedrals but we do need cathedral thinkers, people who can think beyond their own lifetimes, who can glimpse the light beyond the darkness.

Charles Handy's latest book, *The Hungry Spirit*, is published by Arrow.

# Marina Warner

## NECESSARY ANGELS

WHEN ANGELS ARE sighted, as they have been with increasing frequency over the last few years, they take the form of half-dressed shimmering beings 'with wings', the supermarket tabloid *Weekly World News* reported last January, that enable them to hover in midair. The photograph alongside showed a long-limbed, androgynous youth in flight, haloed all over in a glowing envelope of light, one leg in front of the other in a balletic arabesque, the knee uncovered below a short and loosely belted tunic, the wings unfurled, with pinions spread for maximum span – this vision had occurred, the article said, in Dallas, Greensboro, N.Carolina, Illinois, California, and S. Carolina, on at least thirty-five occasions.

Angels today are instantly recognizable – because they inhabit conventions invented by baroque artists in Italy three hundred years ago. They don't have short curls, or wear togas as angels do on early Christian monuments, where they are also usually wingless; they don't wear deacon's liturgical vestments, nor are their wings blazoned with peacock's eyes as in the mosaics and icons of Byzantium; the sweeping long dresses and rainbow plumage of Quattrocento annunciations have been replaced by the accurately represented avian pinions of the Seicento (Caravaggio borrowed a pair of eagle's wings for one of his paintings). They certainly don't sport manly beards, as the visitors to Abraham's table do in some early manuscripts of the Bible. The baroque vision has come to epitomize, even delimit the idea of angels.

To conjure spiritual reality convincingly and communicate a blissful, enraptured, highly emotive metaphysics, artists adapted a visual language of lightness in both senses: radiance and weightlessness. Their angelic visions couldn't take place in the silent and static zone of the two-dimensional picture if they failed to embody them in recognizable and persuasive forms. They couldn't achieve a vivid visual drama of their conjunctions and interactions, could not make us believe in the reality of angels' flight down from the radiant empyrean, or in cherubs gambolling among the clouds unless their iconographical language was stitched into a comprehensible, common web of images and associations.

The effect of baroque airiness is so intrinsic to the work that few people stop incredulously before such paintings to exclaim, 'what a farrago of crackpot fancies', as one does when faced with the latest angelic sighting in California. One achievement of the baroque is its casual, unaffected expression of the fantastic; it makes visible imaginary phenomena as if they had been truly, even routinely experienced with the eyes of the body by both artist and audience. It naturalizes the supernatural with glorious and often joyous engagement: and we, from our post-enlightenment vantage point, may be fortunate enough to be caught up into these ecstatic inventions, however much we resist as sceptics the layered religious and spiritual systems in which they were grown.

*Corpus, non caro* – Body, but not flesh – wrote Saint Augustine when defining the nature of angels. Angels are embodied, but they're not material; and this immateriality presents artists, self-consciously working in a supremely material medium, with their dominant problem. In drawings, you can sometimes see the artist thinking through the difficulties, with a sketch of a naked foot on a pile of studio linen that is standing in for clouds, or of cherubim clustered around a levitating Virgin, laying on her light, angelic handholds so as to waft her skywards, rather than heave her.

Light – both luminousness and vaporousness – buoys this paradoxical, this impossible angelic body, incorporated but not enfleshed, and renders it at once palpable and insubstantial: the lightness of being not so much unbearable, as transcendent. The complexity of angels is unfathomable, but

Harold Bloom, the veteran American literary critic, in his brave, odd book, *Omens of Millennium*, comments: 'It puzzles me that transcendent intimations, once vouchsafed to spiritual adepts and powerful intellects, now seem available mostly to devotees of dank crankeries.' He goes on to explore the history of theological arguments about the nature of angels in the world's great religions, in an attempt to restore philosophy and history to present understanding. In passing he tells that a fifteenth-century bishop managed, after long computation from evidence in the Bible and other sources, to count the number of fallen angels, and decided that Lucifer and his minions numbered exactly 133,306,668.

More seriously, Bloom introduces the Kabbalistic idea that 'every word that is uttered creates an angel'. This was a current belief among Jewish mystics in sixteenth-century Palestine, who also held that when Kabbalists read the Torah, not only the words but the letters and the spaces in between the letters and the words, and interpretations of these gaps also brought forth angels. Bloom argues a subtle, highly contemporary secular position from this idea, that it is indeed language that creates angels; the word becomes flesh through art; thus paintings do not represent phenomena waiting in invisible realms to be made apparent, but generate them, forge them, make them without external or prior referent. Visions don't materialize in painted representations from a prior existence; they don't exist until they're made visible by the image. If baroque painters had not enfleshed angels, angels wouldn't exist – or certainly not as we know them now. As Wallace Stevens writes in his poem *The Necessary Angel*:

Am I not,

Myself only half a figure of a sort,

A figure half seen for a moment, a man
Of the mind, an apparition apparelled in

Apparels of such lightest look that a turn
Of my shoulder and quickly, too quickly, I am gone?

Baroque paintings of angels trumpeting the coming of the
saviour figure forth these 'apparels of such lightest look'.
Through them we see the 'men of the mind', angels who have
been and are such necessary inhabitants of that 'intermediate
realm', as Henri Corbin calls it, that lies 'between the sensory
and the intellectual world . . . one akin to what we call the
imaginings of poets.'

Augustine also said that angels were such by virtue of their
office, not their nature; what they do characterizes them,
more than what they are. They're not static beings, but
energumens, always in the act of becoming, or passing
through, of flying past. They're able to generate the intermediate realm because they are themselves intermediaries,
messengers between worlds, between differences of earth and
heaven, flesh and spirit. *Angelos* (Greek) and *malek* (Hebrew)
both mean messenger, and angels appear to give messages, as
at the Annunciation to Mary or the warning to Joseph of the
massacre of the innocents; they proclaim events (*Hark the
Herald Angels Sing!*); and they perform the office of others,
guarding the gates of Eden with a fiery sword and battling,
like the archangel Michael, with the devil.

Marking passages and passing messages, Christian angels
borrowed, from around the fifth century the features of their
classical counterparts: winged Hermes or Mercury, the god of
journeys, of crossroads and the gods' own messenger, who
wore a cap of invisibility and the first seven league boots of
fairy-tale. Nike, the goddess of Victory, who descends from
the heights as in the famous Victory of Samothrace to crown
the hero, and defines a precise moment in time when fortune
changes, also lent many aspects of her bodily appearance to
angels, though not, in Christian belief her definite feminine
gender. But in the Seicento, artists unequivocally adopted as
their angelic model another divine Olympian: Eros, the god
who has the distinction of appearing twice in Hesiod's
*Theogony*, the most influential genealogy of the gods and

goddesses, for significantly, he appears full-grown at the very beginning of creation itself, as a demiurge, bringing chaos to order, the energy of love represented as the generative force of creation itself. Only later does he take his place in the divine pantheon as the son of Aphrodite, the goddess of love.

For Freud, whose translators naturalized in English the very word eros, the Greeks' envisioning of sexual passion in the form of a beautiful, smiling winged youth effectively, even dazzlingly, materialized that virtual power within human consciousness that Hesiod described:

> Love makes men weak
> He overpowers the clever mind, and tames
> The spirit in the breasts of men and gods.

Freud collected *erotes*, statues of the god, and he also bought several examples of another, rare type of classical Eros, in which he takes the form of a child, neither cupid nor angel, but a mischieveous, barely pubescent and puckish charmer, lifting his tunic to show his genitals with a complicit smile.

Child angels or cupids represent a different, magical order of flesh, neither living nor dead in the human sense, but gravity-free, paradisaically naked, and yet substantial, not so etherealized, but real enough, often, to cast shadows. Such heavenly spirits are also called *amorini*, or *putti*, and in baroque art, where they are omnipresent, they modulate classical ideas of pleasure and love. Neither strictly Christian nor pagan, neither altogether personal subjects nor allegorical personifications, they people the imaginary world of the supernatural as their most characteristic denizens. For they are invoked to make visible a cluster of metaphors to express spirit. Their presence underscores nativity scenes, like a musical motif playing in the background, often almost imperceptibly filling the spaces of sky or the edges of the composition with their weightless, peachy bodies, their child-like, innocent playfulness.

These are most emphatically not the cherubim described in the Old Testament, who appeared to the prophet Ezekiel

(1:16–10), and who have four faces, each of them whorled with four wings, blazoned with eyes, with human hands but calves' hooves and feet of brass; nor are they like the seraphim who stand above the throne of the Lord in the vision of Isaiah (6:1–2). Bodiless heads of cherubs sometimes recall these winged monsters of the Bible, but the Bible's influence on the iconography had become vague and weak by the sixteenth century: angels and *putti* communicate Eros, in his double aspect as both man-youth and man-child, the traditional companion of Aphrodite, who takes the role in myth of her son and errand-boy, as well as of her emanation. Baroque *erote*s materialize in paint the cloud of desire that the goddess of love breathes, entering accents of sinless, spontaneous carnality into sins pious and pagan as they twist and bounce, presenting their plump and rosy rumps and their baby genitals to the spectator with unalloyed delight, replicated and even multiplied throughout the images like so many caresses made palpable.

The indeterminate status of the *putto*, neither particular angel, nor general allegory, enhances their effect in paintings, as visible vitality reproducing its own likenesses by sheer parthenogenetic energy: love breeding love, one kiss following another, angels in a choric role, messengers giving expression to the passions.

But as spirits made visible, the angels who breathe wisdom into chosen mediators, do not shed that first function we looked at, of re-animation: they quicken and transform the seers who receive their messages, and their flight and soaring, their kinetic poses, their arabesques on the diagonal and their *sotto-in-su* acrobatics all reinforce the idea of divine energy in action, of the intervention that can miraculously move and shape and transform matter on the lower plane.

Angels sing in the gospels; they carol at the nativity in medieval illuminations, and in numerous evocations of paradise: for Dante the spheres of heaven themselves ring in harmony to the sound of divine praises. So the musician angels of the baroque period aren't an innovation. However, again, baroque artists introduce, in the naked, intimate,

51

mingled and sometimes even hoydenish limbs of their singers and players, the strains of a pent-up blissfulness that is very different from the decorous choruses evoked by Fra Angelico, or by Piero della Francesca, for example. Ludovico Carracci's band of angel musicians lean in voluptuously towards one another, and one of them appears to be a girl, with breasts uncovered, while the singers below in the distance meld together in an golden summery afterglow, around the score held high. The scene recalls Schumann's later metaphor for the *lied* itself: 'the child grew wings', as these choristers breathe out, ex-spire in order to breathe into us, in-spire us, to catch us up into their dimensions of ecstasy. Viol players sitting on the clouds of heaven sometimes look out at us invitingly from baroque paintings, often showing a single leg, in the asymmetrical straddling position that characterises the mobility and restless energy of the baroque body.

But again, mediating ideas of spirit or breath, of souls rising, these child-angels and young androgyne angels sublimate the erotic, tap its energies to dematerialize the embodied anthropomorphic forms with which representational picturing has to work. The singing voices and the sound of viols and pipes and organs, transport the onlooker into their acoustic range, another place, a disembodied, unearthly zone that cannot be seen and can be reached through hearing from far far away. It's not just the children that grow wings; we are allowed to as well, as we look – to join in their flight into those dizzy baroque spaces of light and air. We can taste artists' dreams of paradisaical bliss when we enter their invented worlds, where angels fly, sing and play on the viol.

Marina Warner's latest book,
*No Go the Bogeyman*, is published
by Chatto & Windus.

# Alison Weir

## CHRISTMAS AT THE COURT OF HENRY VIII

'PASTIME WITH GOOD company, I love and shall until I die,' wrote the young King Henry VIII, whose court was renowned throughout Christendom for its splendour and entertainments. Each year, the annual routine of that court culminated in December in the twelve days of merrymaking that constituted a Tudor Christmas, although the King's celebrations were naturally immensely more lavish than those of most of his subjects.

Henry VIII usually kept Christmas at Greenwich, in the Thames-side palace in which he had been born. With precedent and custom dictating the course and nature of the proceedings, which echoed the time-honoured traditions of the late medieval court, King Henry celebrated the birth of Christ with 'much nobleness and open court'.

Christmas Eve was a fast day, a day given over to final preparations such as decorating the great hall with boughs of ivy, bay and holme (evergreen oak) and bringing in the mighty Yule Log, which would burn in the hearth of the hall throughout the twelve days of the season 'to the great rejoicing of the Queen and the nobles'. After the festivities had come to an end, the charred remains of the Yule Log would be kept and used to light its successor the following year. Traditionally on Christmas Eve, mummers would perform a play depicting the legend of St George and the Dragon.

Christmas Day was a holy day devoted to acts of worship

and a solemn banquet in honour of the Nativity; it was the days that followed that were given over to feasting and 'disports'. It was incumbent upon kings and nobles to dispense hospitality throughout the season, and the doors of the court were thrown open to the public, who were allowed in to watch the 'goodly and gorgeous mummeries' from a safe distance and partake of the festive fare that was distributed among them.

Each season, a Lord of Misrule, or 'master of merry disports', was elected. Adorned with scarves, ribbons, laces, jewels and bells, mounted on a hobby horse, and escorted by pipers and drummers, his job was to act as master of ceremonies. He was solemnly crowned and was allowed to choose servants to wait upon him. Often, he carried out his duties boisterously and noisily, with little respect for the demands of etiquette. Will Wynesbury was Lord of Misrule at Henry's first Yuletide as King, and impudently asked his sovereign for five pounds towards his expenses, which amused Henry inordinately. It is clear that distinctions of rank were relaxed at Christmastime.

More than a thousand people dined at court during the Christmas season. An Italian visitor wrote: 'The guests remained at table for seven hours. The removal and replacing of dishes was incessant, the hall in every direction being full of fresh viands on the way to table.' The food served was rich and varied, and included 'every imaginable sort of meat known in the kingdom, and fish in like manner, even down to prawn pasties'.

The chief dishes were roast peacock, served in its reserved skin and glorious plumage, and the traditional boar's head, dressed with herbs and with an apple in its mouth; the Boar's Head carol was first printed during Henry VIII's reign. All meats were carried into the banqueting hall with due ceremony; far from conforming to the chicken-throwing image portrayed by Charles Laughton, the table manners of the King and his courtiers were refined and decorous, following a strict code of etiquette. As for dessert, the jellies of twenty sorts surpassed everything, being made in the shape of castles and animals, as beautiful as can be imagined'. Frumenty – a mixture of wheat or corn boiled in milk with fruit and even meat – was extremely popular, and would one day evolve into our Christmas pudding. Throughout each meal, minstrels would play in the gallery.

The entertainments for the Christmas season, as for other celebrations, were organized by the Master of the Revels, who kept so many elaborate costumes and props that he had to be provided with large storerooms. These entertainments usually took the form of pageants, disguisings and masques, the latter being an Italian novelty introduced into England during the Twelfth Night entertainments of 1511 by William Cornish, Master of the Children of the Chapel Royal. The masque, which thereafter proved very popular, combined music, song and pageantry with intricate dances; the players wore allegorical costume, and members of the audience were invited to join in. Henry VIII, who was an excellent dancer, often took part, usually in disguise.

Pageants were elaborate tableaux with allegorical or symbolic meaning; those taking part would recite laudatory verses, and the whole object of the exercise was to achieve a breathtaking spectacle. Disguisings, much beloved by Henry himself, involved the King and his nobles appearing in disguise, often as emissaries from exotic lands or legendary characters such as Robin Hood and his Merry Men, then joining a banquet or picnic, and engaging the courtiers in discourse and dancing before unmasking to the general – and predictable – surprise of everyone.

Other Christmas pastimes included dancing and singing carols in the great hall: carols were not exclusively Christmas songs at this time, but were sung at all seasons of the year, and were still performed in their original form, as a round dance. Board games such as chess and backgammon were played at court, while gambling with cards and dice was very popular, and was organized by the Knight Marshal of the Household. The game of Mumchance, played for high stakes, often rounded off a court banquet.

New Year's Day, rather than Christmas Day itself, was

when gifts were exchanged according to a long-established ritual. In the morning, the Usher of the Chamber would stand in the open doorway of the royal bedchamber and announce that His Majesty was ready for the bringing in of the gifts. Outside, servants and present-givers waited in line with their offerings, while inside the bedchamber, the royal family would have gathered, the King sitting at the foot of his bed.

The ritual words were the same each year.

'Sire,' the Usher would cry, 'here is a New Year's gift coming from the Queen.'

'Let it come in, Sir,' the King would reply, and the Queen's gift would be brought in, followed by gifts from every member of the court, in order of rank. Then the Queen would be presented with her gifts, and the royal children theirs. In turn, the King would give presents to his family and favoured members of his court.

The celebrations reached their climax on Twelfth Night, the Feast of the Epiphany, which marked the coming of the Magii to Bethlehem, and on that evening a sumptuous banquet would mark the end of the Yuletide season. The Steward of the Household would bring in the wassail bowl, crying, 'Wassail! Wassail! Wassail!', to which the Children of the Chapel Royal would respond with 'a good song'. There were disguisings in the torchlit hall, which was always hung with tapestries in honour of the occasion. After the disguisings, spiced wine (hippocras), wafers and sweets were served to the King and Queen and their courtiers.

Alison Weir's latest book,
*Elizabeth the Queen*, is
published by Jonathan Cape.

# Nigella Lawson

## Food for the Festival of Lights

HANUKAH IS THE Jewish Festival of Lights, an eight-day affair which tends to fall in December and has thus been appropriated as a kind of *yiddisher* Christmas by Jewish Americans who want to show they've got their own party to go to as well. It is, in fact, no such thing, but rather a small – admittedly significant – commemoration of the victory of the Maccabees in 165BC. Anyway, it was the American Jews who invented Christmas as we now think of and celebrate it: that's to say the Hollywood version; it was, after all, Irving Berlin who wrote 'White Christmas'. Hanukah is something entirely different, far more low key.

Actually, I have never celebrated it; any knowledge I have is recent and book-learnt. I had a perfectly respectable Jewish atheist upbringing which managed seamlessly to incorporate Christmas and all its pomps: stockings, advent calenders, baubles, carols, turkey – the full *shmeer*. Indeed, my great-grandmother was so keen on Christmas lunch that she had it twice: once, unremarkably, on the 25th December; with a reprise on Midsummer Day, a kind of Sydney Christmas in London.

I can't celebrate Hanukah: it would be false; I would feel uncomfortable. This may partly be due to that peculiarly British upper-middle-class form of Jewish anti-semitism in which I was immersed at an early age. But more, I feel, it is because you can't acquire rituals – any more than you can acquire nicknames – by decision alone. My rituals, illogical as it may be, are the rituals of Christmas; those are my childhood memories. Anything else feels like affectation or the stiff accommodation of a culture which cannot but feel – blood notwithstanding – alien.

I am being irrational, of course: it doesn't really make sense to adopt one religion's rituals without feeling it necessary to adopt the faith to go with it, but to reject another's on the grounds that I am unable to respond with any accompanying and comfortable spiritual adherence. But because I was brought up to see the Christmas paraphernalia as culturally neutral – which in a sense it is – I can't always see the extent of the problem; I am, though, more aware of the discrepancy, a slight, itching lack of resolution, now that I have children of my own. Or, rather, it is more the case that I have been made to see it. Last year, my husband got furious when I bought my daughter a Barbie Advent Calender. In truth, as I explained to him, Christians had rather more right than Jews to be offended by it. Displaying Barbie in fetching pose with fur hat and muff, against a swirling Doctor Zhivago-esque snow-storm, this was an artefact wholly devoid of Christian connotation. But I got his point, even if I wasn't swayed by it. I see that some sort of accommodation has to be made; and I plan to eat my way out of it – or rather, into it. Just as I like Christmas for the food, so I think the way to incorporate Hanukah, authentically, is culinarily.

Hanukah is called the Festival of the Lights because – the story goes – when, after the Maccabean victory, the Jews returned to Jerusalem, they found that the pagans had desecrated the temple, polluted the oil and stopped all but one oil-lamp from burning. There was only enough oil to let it burn for one more day, and the Jews duly lit it and it continued to burn for eight, allowing them time to clean the temple and replenish their supplies of holy oil. The miracle of the oil is celebrated culinarily by using it in great vats in which to dunk, splutteringly, latkes, doughnuts, batter-wrapped pieces of chicken, fritters. The Jewish genius is to turn a religious festival into a divine ordinance to eat fried food.

Eating latkes – desirably stodgy potato cakes, which I like with cold meats but are perhaps best eaten alone, palateskinningly hot with cold, cinnamon-infused apple purée dolloped on top – is the commonest British way of marking the occasion. Push about 2kg of potatoes, peeled, through the grater disc of the food processor. Remove and drain in a sieve, pushing well to remove all excess liquid. Then fit the double-bladed knife and put a peeled medium-sized onion, coarsely chopped, three eggs, a teaspoon of salt, some pepper and about four tablespoons of self-raising flour (or matzo meal, which is better according to my mother-in-law) in the bowl and process briefly. Then add the grated potatoes and give a quick pulse till the mixture is pulpy but not totally puréed. This should be a thick sticky mess; if it is at all runny add more flour.

Fry the latkes in lumps – about a tablespoon of the mixture for each – in a heavy based frying pan with hot oil bubbling away in it to a depth of about 1.25 cm. About five minutes a side should do it, maybe even less.

Edda Servi Machlin, in her resonant, necessarily elegiac, book, *The Classic Cuisine of the Italian Jews* writes of her aunt's *frittelle di chanukà*, yeasty, diamond-shaped dough-nuts fried till golden and then drenched in a lemon and honey syrup. I love anything made of batter, any form of doughnut. But it's the Greek version loukamades (eaten all over Greece, in fact, all year round and regardless of ethnicity) which have the virtue, too, of not being yeast-leavened and therefore requiring less time to make, which I plan to make part of our family ritual. They are, in fact, not really doughnuts, but spoonfuls of choux pastry, deep fried and then rolled, straight out of the fiercely hot oil, in a chilled aromatic syrup. Make them and hand out to waiting children, kept at a safe distance (especially at this fraught time of year, which is perhaps not ideally suited to bouts of deep-frying). Whatever and for whoever: to be eaten straight away and with fingers.

## LOUKAMADES

for the choux pastry fritters:

100g plain flour
175ml water
75g unsalted butter, diced
pinch salt
2 large eggs, beaten

for the syrup:

500ml water
400g sugar
1 stick of cinnamon
1 teasp orange flower water

for frying:

about 1 litre olive (or vegetable) oil

You can make the syrup in advance if you like. Put the sugar and water and cinnamon stick in a saucepan and slowly bring to the boil. When it starts boiling and the sugar has dissolved turn up the heat and let it bubble ferociously for about 7 minutes. Add the orange flower water and give it another minute or three. What you want is a syrup that isn't exactly runny, but isn't honey-thick either, for it will thicken as it cools. Don't panic about it, though: too thick or too thin, it will still work, still taste wonderful. And it's impossible to give precise timings: so much depends on your hob, the size of the pan, what it's made of; for what it's worth, the above timings are based on an 18cm pan. Pour the syrup into a jug or bowl to cool and remove the cinnamon stick. Now, you will have a lot of syrup, but that's because I like a lot: I want these doughnuts *swimming* in it. If your tastes are more austere, make less.

Now for the loukamades. Pour the oil for frying into a wide-ish pan to come up to about 4cm. I specify, first, olive oil, because it is, in this context, the holy oil; the one that went on burning miraculously. Of course, substitute vegetable oil if you want, but it isn't *echt*. If you're using olive oil it shouldn't be extra virgin: just the ordinary, light golden, faster flowing (and cheaper) stuff. I put the oil on for frying before I make the choux pastry, but you could do it the other way round if it makes you panic less. But in that case, keep the dough covered until you use it. In my pan (which is 23cm in diameter and 7cm deep – for safety, it should really be deeper) the oil takes a good 20 minutes to get hot enough for deep-frying so there's no rush. Just make sure you've got everything weighed out and to hand before you start.

Sieve the flour. Put the water and butter and salt in a decent-sized saucepan on the hob and heat until the butter has melted and the water begun to boil. Take the pan immediately off the heat (you don't want the water to evaporate at all) and beat in the flour. Use a wooden spoon for this and don't worry about how lumpy it is or how unyielding, just keep beating until it comes smoothly – still thickly – together. A minute or so should do it. Put the pan back on the heat for just long enough to finish this process off – about a minute or even less – until the dough begins to come away from the sides of the pan to form a smooth ball.

Now you beat in the eggs, and you can either do this by hand (not difficult but you'll need muscle-power) or by machine. So, either turn the dough into a mixing bowl and add spoonfuls of egg as you continue to beat with your wooden spoon or turn it into the bowl of a food processor fitted with the double-blade and pour, gradually, the eggs through the funnel while blitzing. You may not need all of the eggs, so go carefully, until you have a smooth, gleaming dough, soft but still stiff enough to hold its shape. Be prepared, too, to add another egg if needed. You want to be able to dip a teaspoon into the mixture (and dip this teaspoon in oil first to stop the dough sticking) and then, with a finger push it off the spoon into the fat; so it mustn't be runny.

The oil should be almost at smoking point and you can watch the fritters swell up and grow golden as they cook. I find four minutes does them (and I cook four to five at a time). But just taste as you go along (make that sacrifice) to check the insides are soft but cooked, rather than still doughy. As you remove – with one of those fine-meshed stock de-scummers for preference – the spiky little doughnut balls from the pan (and at this heat the oil will not make the fritters greasy so no need to start faffing about with kitchen paper towels) put them immediately on a waiting plate and spoon over syrup and continue to roll them in it. In fact, this is best done by a pair of you: the one to cook the loukamades; the other to ladle over the syrup and then roll them assiduously in the syrup.

Makes about 30. Enjoy.

Nigella Lawson's latest book, *How to Eat: The Pleasures and Principles of Good Food*, is published by Chatto & Windus.

# Sara Wheeler

## CAMPING IN ANTARCTICA

WHEN THE STORM ended, the world seemed new, and the huts shed their extra cladding of ice like the ark dripping water. The snow had been blown from the foothills of Erebus, revealing polished blue ice stuck fast to the rock which here and there protruded like an elbow below the treacherously seductive crevasse fields. A thin band of apricot and petrol-blue hung over the Transantarctics, and the pallid sun shed a watery light over thousands of miles of ice. The frozen Sound could have been the silent corner of the African savannah where man first stood upright.

The storm seemed to have blanched our interior landscapes too. We sat outside in the evening calm. Often we saw nacreous clouds then, drifting high up in the infinite reaches of the sky – about ten miles up, actually, far higher than the fluffy white clouds at home that send down rain. There might be twenty-five of them, in twenty-five variations of opalescent lemons, rich reds and reedy greens. They were brightest just after sunset, when the glare of the sun had disappeared at ground level, but its light still illuminated high clouds. The nacreous clouds were small, oval and quite separate one from the other, and they floated along in a line like fat, iridescent pearls on an invisible thread. As Gertrude Stein said, 'Paradise – if you can stand it.' The dignity of the landscape infused our minds like a symphony; I heard another music in those days.

I hiked up towards Lake Chad, following the route I had taken to the Bonney camp with Ed, the mountaineering physicist the previous summer. The ice was cracking like a whip on tin. Sometimes, out of the corner of my eye, I caught a white bolt of lightning flashing across the chalky blue. Of course, I knew this landscape. But I had never seen the pink glow of dawn over the Canada Glacier, or the panoply of sunset over the Suess, or, in between, sunlight travelling from one peak to the next and never coming down to us on the lake. We lived in a bowl of shadow for those days. One morning the sun appeared for ten minutes in the cleft between the Canada and the mountain next to it, and the scientists stopped working to look up. The lake was carpeted with compacted snow, and from the middle, where the Canada came tumbling down in thick folds, the Suess was cradled by mountains like a cup of milky liquid.

On our last night, Lucia had gone outside after dinner to empty the dishwater into its drum. Suddenly she appeared at the hut window, gesticulating furiously. I rushed out, thinking perhaps that the propane toilet had exploded again. But it wasn't that. She was looking up at the electric gallery of the southern lights. The sky was streaked with faint emerald shadows, splaying out in several directions to the horizon, changing shape, spreading, and bleeding into the blackness. Iridescent coppery beams roamed among the stars like searchlights, and soft ruby flames flickered gently above the glacier, sporadically leaping forward into the middle of the dark sky. Towards the east, a rich and luminous topaz haze rolled lazily back and forwards like a tide. At one point the whole sky was a rainbow, flaming with radiant mock suns.

'Heavenly music,' I murmured.

Sara Wheeler is the author of *Terra Incognita:
Travels in Antarctica*, published
by Vintage.

# Frances Wilks

## A Light Christmas

WHEN I WAS little we lived in Malaya (it actually *was* Malaya then). A large promontory of jungle-clad land pointed down to the nearby equator. The spinal column of mountains down its back were covered in jungles so seemingly impenetrable that I believed them to be full of tigers. I was told that, if you carried an umbrella when walking in the jungle, it could save your life. The trick was to open the umbrella incredibly slowly so that the tiger would become mesmerised and wouldn't pounce. (I accepted this as gospel truth until fairly recently.)

Penang, where we were, was a little island casually flung off the western coastline of Malaya's big body. It was hot in Penang all the year round, except in the hot season, when it got even hotter. The rest of the time it was a relentless eighty-nine degrees Fahrenheit. One day a year, it was said, it was just cool enough to wear a woolly. As well as the heat, there was an intensely bright, almost painful quality to the sunlight, pretty well unknown in temperate climes, at least until the advent of global warming. The noonday light bleached the colour out of everything.

Christmas was wedged in at the end of the monsoon just before the beginning of the seriously hot season. Preparing for Christmas was great fun. My mother, a very resourceful woman, had childhood memories of holly, mistletoe, mince pies and roaring log fires. She was determined to recreate some of the magic of an English Christmas for me, even if it meant a degree of artifice. 'Let's go round to the back of the island and see if we can find a wild tree that has leaves a bit like holly,' she said enthusiastically the week before Christmas. Recently, joyfully, out of school, I accompanied her in the large green Wolseley that she drove around the island with careless precision. Sure enough a suitable tree was found. The leaves were larger and less spiky than real holly leaves and they had emerald tints rather than being a uniform bottle green. But no matter, it was near enough.

On the way home, I begged to go to the Monkey Gardens. These were an early, colonial version of a safari park, a drive-through with monkeys instead of lions. The monkeys were marvellously playful. Just for the hell of it, they would climb on board and twang the aerial of a passing vehicle or snap the elastic of a windscreen wiper.

Back at home, my mother and I experimented with wax to make berries for our tropical holly. We melted down candles in the oven and when the wax was still warm and malleable, rolled them into little rounds. Then we put them in the fridge to harden. First we started with white candles, intending to paint them. But then we had a breakthrough. If we used red candles, the berries would emerge ready-coloured. Next we had to attach the berries to the fake holly. I think we used green wire, which we wrapped tightly around the holly stem and then pierced the free end into the heart of the wax berry.

Waking up on Christmas morning was always tremendously exciting. Because Penang is so close to the equator, there are always twelve hours a day and twelve hours a night. (Even after living in England for thirty years, I find our huge seasonal variation in light rather tiring. Just when you have got used to it being dark at a certain time, it changes.) I knew as a child that, if I woke at dawn, it was always six o'clock. But I used to wake earlier than that on Christmas mornings. Quite often I would find a sleeping adult in the twin bed next to mine. As we had no formal guestroom a friend of my parents would often doss down there; too tired or drunk after a dinner party to make it home.

I didn't know if the sleeping, tossing form was a man or a woman – it didn't seem to matter. Slowly and carefully, I felt at the end of my bed for my Christmas sack of presents. Not wishing to disturb my unknown roommate's dreams, I tried to unwrap the little parcels in the dark as noiselessly as possible. By touch alone I would detect their form, characteristics and likely use. One year, I unwrapped a whole tin hospital in the dark. The mass of the structure defeated my seven-year-old skills of classification but the individual patients and pieces of equipment excited me. There were stretchers and wheelchairs which provoked whole scenarios in my imagination with operations, recovery rooms, convalescences and the mysterious 'going home'. For a child who had had less than their fair share of illness, I was morbidly interested in the experience of disease.

With the arrival of daylight, the brightly painted hospital was revealed in its full glory. Three floors, with an interconnecting hand-powered lift. Perspex screens which could be used to section off areas, as additional ward space was needed for urgent cases. A whole series of immaculate nurses stood poised to take up their duties. Serious looking doctors consulted with *gravitas*. The patients, some prone, and clearly very ill, some just well enough to sit up, some just taking their first, tremulous steps after a long time being bedridden – all awaited my healing touch to put the drama in motion. Not for nothing is the place where operations are carried out called an operating *theatre*. It is a point of pride with me that nobody ever died in my hospital although some were dangerously close to it. We just managed to pull them back from the brink with a heroic flourish.

After the excitement of the sack of presents, the rest of the day was an attempt at a Northern European Christmas. C of E church in the morning, with an incomprehensible sermon about 'snow in midwinter'. Then an improbably large Christmas lunch, a roast with all the trimmings. Turkeys were virtually unknown there then so a large chicken played substitute. A Christmas Pudding was faked up out of ice-cream and fruit and brandy. In later years I would come to recognize it as rum and raisin ice-cream – which can be eaten at any time of the year and has no longer any festive overtones.

By the end of Christmas day the wax holly-berries, so crisp when taken out of the icy recesses of the fridge that morning, would start to wilt. At first they would lose their circularity and then start to droop into elongated Gaudiesque shapes. A traditional Christmas couldn't last long in that level of heat and light. Boxing Day was business as usual. A trip to the Penang swimming pool, the only place to get really cool apart from an air-conditioned room, or a walk up Penang Hill, where the altitude offered some respite from the heat. On the walk up there was a government water tank brimmingly full of chill springwater. My parents used to test their friends' shockability level by suggesting a skinny-dip in it and noting their reactions.

When I arrived 'back home' in England at the age of ten I couldn't wear shoes or an overcoat for weeks. They seemed too restricting. Everything was alien, cold and dark. I noticed particularly the lack of light in the long winter months. Used to the constant brilliant light I found it unbelievable that days could pass by without sight of the sun. Nervously I approached my first English Christmas.

Everyone else seemed to enjoy the rituals and to feel that this was what Christmas was all about. A series of Christmas puddings were made and steamed seemingly for days. The shops were full of real Christmas paraphernalia which required no adjustments. On the actual day itself, guests and relations sat around stiffly, over-eating and somehow rooted to the spot. I was bewildered. This wasn't Christmas. Christmas was about an imaginative act of faking, of creatively making substitutes and having fun doing it. By contrast the real thing seemed dull.

I suggested to my father that Christmas should be moved to the middle of summer, when at least people could have a good time with their windows and doors open and the possibility of going out into the garden. 'It would be warm and sunny then.' He thought about it for a long time and then said, 'But the point about Christmas is that it does come at the worst time of the year, just after the shortest day, when we're at our lowest ebb in terms of light. Before the days of Christianity, people used to have a festival at the winter solstice in order to give themselves hope. Christmas is really about remembering that there is the possibility of light in the deepest darkness.'

Frances Wilks's latest book,
*Intelligent Emotion*, is published
by Heinemann.

# Leslie Kenton

## CHILD OF LIGHT

'YOUR CHILDREN ARE not your children,' wrote the Lebanese poet Kihil Kenton, 'they are the sons and daughters of Life's longing for itself ... You are the bows from which your children as living arrows are sent forth.' It is a quote I like, not only because – having raised four children on my own –I believe it to be just about the most accurate description of parenthood I have ever come across, but also because it emphasizes the 'lightness' which develops when you give up trying to be perfect and come to trust the processes of Nature. Each child that comes into the world is a being of light who has chosen for a time to crystallize its soul in the form of a human body. So much of a child's truth and beauty gets destroyed by us, by our forgetting that the light which children bring into the world will transform our own lives and remind us that we too are light beings – if only we will let it happen.

My first child was born in a huge teaching hospital in Los Angeles. The labour was long and regrettably not natural. I was given an analgesic during labour and an epidural for the delivery. It was all very cold, efficient and mechanical. Because the hospital I was in happened to be a Catholic one in which every other woman there seemed already to know the ropes since she was giving birth to her fifth or eighth or tenth child – nobody bothered to tell me much about what was going on or what was expected of me. My baby was taken from me immediately after the birth and put into a nursery with all of the other babies while I was wheeled off to a private room. Soon they brought this tiny creature to me. I held him in my arms and stared at him in stark wonder. Then at three hourly intervals he would reappear for twenty minutes at a time and I'd hold him in bed beside me until the nurse would come and take him away again. The third or fourth time they brought him to me, he began to cry. I nestled him, rocked him, and spoke gently to him but he wouldn't stop so I rang for the nurse.

'My baby's crying,' I said. 'What should I do?'

'Have you burped him?'

'Burped him?'

'You *have* fed him haven't you?'

'Fed him? Am I supposed to feed him?'

The nurse took him and put him to my breast. His tiny mouth opened and reached for me as if he had known for ever what to do. He began to suck with such force it took my breath away. It was like being attached to a vacuum cleaner. I began to laugh. I couldn't help myself. It seemed incredible that such a tiny creature could have such power and determination. He too had a purpose. He was raw, insistent and real. With every fibre of his being, this child was drawing his life and he would not be denied.

Tears of joy ran shamelessly down my cheeks while he sucked. There in the midst of all that clinical green and white, I had discovered what love was all about. It was really quite simple – a meeting of two beings. The age, the sex, the relationship didn't matter. That day – two creatures – he and I – had met. We touched each other in utter honesty and simplicity. There was nothing romantic or solemn about it. No obligations, no duties, no fancy games, and you didn't have to read an encyclopedia of baby care to experience it. We'd met – just that. Somewhere in spirit we were friends. I knew beyond all doubt that I had found something real and real it has remained.

Children make the greatest teachers when we are willing to enter their worlds, lay aside our preconceived ideas and learn about how each of them views life. Looking at the world through the eyes of a child transforms humdrum reality into a magical land of the unexpected. It can also teach you a lot about how your child thinks and grows emotionally. 'Cigars are fattening,' my eight-year-old son Jesse announced one day. 'I know because all the men who smoke them are fat.'

Children have incredible wit and freshness. Everything is new to them. The most trivial event can bring to a child the kind of pleasure we adults spend a lot of money searching for. But that's not all. In subtle ways, they are able to teach us truths that we might otherwise never learn. Once, when we were experiencing gale-force winds, five-year-old Jesse sat at the window watching what the wind did to the trees. Finally he turned to me and said, 'Reflexible trees are stronger than ordinary trees. Do you think reflexible people are stronger than other people?' I was slow to answer as I couldn't imagine what he was talking about. 'Jesse, what are reflexible trees?' I asked. 'They're the kind that bend all the way to the ground when the wind blows instead of pushing against it,' he said. 'The reflexible ones don't get cracked like the others.' 'Yes,' I replied, 'I guess you're right. Reflexible trees and reflexible people really are stronger than the rest.'

Through thirty-eight years of motherhood, plus years working with young children in nursery school, I have never stopped learning from them. I know it is supposed to be the other way around – and I have always done my best to explain the intricacies of life to my children and pupils – but in the meantime they have taught me lessons I won't soon forget: lessons in courtesy, humour, responsibility. They have shown me how to be angry and how to forgive, how to care for another and still demand my own right to separateness. Most of all, through knowing and watching them, I've begun learning how to live – an art that, on too many occasions during these years, I had almost forgotten.

Children have also taught me much of what I know about love. They have a singularly unsentimental attitude towards love and show little patience with an adult's romantic notions. To a child love is nothing fancy. It is a real and tangible feeling to be taken highly seriously. 'If you love somebody,' a six-year-old boy named Charlie once told me, 'then you help him put his boots on when they get stuck.' 'When I grow up,' said eight-year-old Marlene, 'I'm going to love somebody even if his handwriting is messy.'

I once had a real demonstration of what love is all about

from my eldest son, Branton, who was then eight and to all appearances totally indifferent to his little sister, Susannah. One autumn evening, after we'd all been out in the yard, we discovered Susannah was missing. Through a series of misunderstandings she thought we'd gone off for a walk in the wood – and we thought she'd gone back to the house. By the time I realized she was gone, Branton had a dachshund under each arm and was firmly ensconced on the sofa watching his favourite television programme with a friend. If one thing was certain in our house, it was that Branton would do absolutely nothing anyone wanted him to do – such as set the table or wash his hands – while this particular programme was on. I could stand in the middle of the room and scream at the top of my lungs but he wouldn't hear me.

After I'd searched every room for Susannah, I began to be frightened. It was dark by then, and she was only five years old. Our house in the country had enormous expanses of land and woods surrounding it. She could have been anywhere. Careful not to betray my anxiety, I announced, 'Branton, Susannah is gone.' There was a pause, rather like a slow take in a cartoon film, then he turned and looked at me. 'I can't find Susannah,' I repeated. 'She isn't in the house, and I don't know where she is.'

He was up as if dynamite had blown him off the sofa. The poor sleepy dachshunds were shaken out of their stupor. 'I'll find her,' he said on his way to the door. Then he stopped and turned to his friend, still engrossed in the television programme. 'Get up, Jeff,' he commanded, 'we've got to find Susu. Hurry up.' I have never seen any human being move faster. Within two minutes he had been around the acre of land surrounding the house and rung two doorbells to ask if the neighbours knew where his sister was. By then I had remembered our talk about going for a walk in the woods, and had headed toward the thicket. Branton, still running at top speed, came up and passed me by, all the time calling: 'Susannah, Susannah.'

As we headed up the big path into the woods, I heard the faraway sound of a child crying out. It was Susannah. I tried to reassure her we were coming – while attempting to avoid falling in the wet mud – meanwhile Branton plunged on ahead, apparently afraid of nothing. In another minute he had her in his arms. As I approached, I heard him saying over and over, 'Oh, Susu, Susu, are you all right?' as tears streamed down his cheeks.

Later that night at the dinner table I told Susannah, who frequently suffered Branton's scorn, that now she knew what Branton really felt about her. I suggested she remember this evening whenever she became discouraged by his taunts – calling her a drip, for instance. She smiled. 'You're a drip,' said Branton.

Children have also taught me to express anger and not be afraid of it. Watch two children fight. They sling the most appalling insults at each other. One gives the other a whack and swears not to play with him or her again. Two hours later they are best friends once more. They know so much better than we do how to forgive. Somehow they will seem to understand that being angry with someone, no matter how important it seems at the time, is not half as interesting as all the things you can do, see, say and make together as soon as the anger has passed.

One day in summer, everything seemed to go wrong for me. For no apparent reason I awakened in the morning with the awful feeling that nothing was worthwhile. At 10 a.m. I received a telegram from a publisher saying that two manuscripts (of which I had no copies) had been lost in the mail. By noon not even the brilliance of California sunshine (where we were on holiday the time) could shake off the heavy black cloud that surrounded me. I was angry with myself – and trying to avoid being angry with everyone else. My two younger children, Jesse, aged eight, and Susannah, ten, kept asking me to take them to the beach. I didn't want to go anywhere, especially the beach. I did not want to do anything for anyone. Finally, in the worst possible spirit, I consented – making sure, of course, that they realised I was doing them a big favour.

The pure white sand and the fresh sea air on the almost deserted beach did nothing to improve my mood. It seemed to me that life was 'out there' and I was 'in here' locked away in the depths of the gloomy dungeon I'd built and was powerless to break out of. As the sun shone brighter and more beautiful, I grew steadily more gloomy. Finally I could stand it no longer.

Despite the fact that the children were playing in the sand nearby and I didn't want to upset them, I broke down and cried. Susannah asked what was wrong. 'I don't know, just about everything seems wrong at the moment,' I whined. 'I feel like that sometimes,' Jesse said, offering no sympathy whatsoever. 'I think you must be angry.' 'So what if I am?' I snapped. 'Why don't you hit something?' he suggested. 'There's nothing to hit,' I replied irritably, 'and anyway that's stupid.' 'No, it's not,' Susannah chimed in. 'It will make you feel ever so much better, Mummy. Or maybe you could growl like a dog.'

I was willing to try anything. So, feeling like a complete fool and admonishing myself for behaving so stupidly in front of my own children, I growled and complained. I hated everyone, I said. I hated myself. I was lonely and I felt the whole world was stupid. Then I growled some more while the two of them sat listening silently. Not once did they try to console me, or tell me I was wrong or protest that the world was really a lovely place to love. Not once did they pass judgement on me or make me feel ashamed of myself or foolish. They just sat and waited.

Finally I felt a little better. Jesse had been right, I thought, but I still had no idea where to go from here. At last I was quiet. Only then did Susannah say, 'I think maybe I know what's wrong with you.' 'What?' I asked sceptically. 'You're always thinking about such serious things. You're always telling yourself what to do and what not to do. No wonder you're angry. You've forgotten how to have fun, Mummy.'

She was certainly right. Having fun seemed as far away as the moon at that moment. I realised then, that for several months I had saddled myself with my work as if work were the only thing that mattered. I'd hated almost every minute of it but had felt proud of being such a 'responsible adult'. 'Maybe you're right,' I replied. 'But how does somebody who's forgotten something so important remember it?' 'Come on, let's dig a hole,' was her reply. 'Yeah, I like holes,' Jesse chimed in.

Feeling like a half-frozen hippopotamus, I lifted myself off the towel and mechanically moved towards the site they'd chosen for the hole. I started to dig. Jesse, who tended to act a bit of a clown, was soon sliding down into it and Susannah was snapping at him for 'ruining the shape'. I looked at the two of them fiercely sneering at each other and saw myself as I had been just a few minutes before. I began to laugh. So did they.

Before long we had a beautiful hole dug. It was probably the most beautiful hole you've ever seen . . . or so it seemed to me. We had a contest to see who was best at running up and leaping over it. Then we drew pictures in the sand and ran into the ice-cold water, splashing each other. By the time the first wave struck me, I, like the two of them, had become part of the sea and the sky. There was no more gloom and no more supercilious self-assurances that I was 'doing the best thing'. I was alive again.

Later that evening I thanked Jesse and Susannah for helping me and teaching me to have fun again. Then in typical adult fashion, I added, 'You know I'm likely to forget and be all grumbly again before long.' 'That's all right,' replied Susannah, 'we'll remind you.'

And they have – again and again over the years I have come to know the light that radiates from each human soul through my friendships with children. Now my last child will soon leave school. He is about to make that final shift towards adulthood. And for the first time in almost 40 years of being a mother, I shall be childless. I pause to look back at all I have learned from the light of children. And I smile.

Leslie Kenton is the author of several books, including *New Ageless Ageing* and *Passage to Power*, published by Vermilion.

# John Diamond

## Lit Up

It's a strange thing, and I hadn't thought about it for years, but now you come to mention it, yes: I have seen the light. Or to be more accurate, light is what I saw. But for a moment there it had much the same effect as the genuine experience. Or would have, if I'd let it.

It was Christmas Eve, which was appropriate enough, and I'd been to a carol service with my friends, and then we'd all gone out and got drunk. Irreligious? Possibly, but don't tell me about it: tell them. I'm Jewish. We're allowed to get drunk on Christmas Eve. I'm not suggesting it's actively encouraged, of course, but I don't think there's any specific talmudic proscription against it. Whatever: we'd spent a couple of hours singing about how Meek and Mild Gentle Jesus is and how 'We Three Kings of Orient' are and so on, the words of which I sang with rather more certainty than I could have brought to its Jewish equivalent, and then we'd spent a couple more hours in the Horse and Wells, and I was walking home in that rolling way you do when you're content with your drunkenness because you know you can sleep it off uninterrupted the next day.

Which is when I saw the fiery red cross burning in the dark sky, above a range of scrubby heathland, its outline twitching slightly as the wind whipped the branches of the trees on that western fringe of the Epping Forest across it. I couldn't tell how big it was, or how near: there was nothing visible around it in the dark to give it a context, but it was a substantial sort of thing, ten or fifteen or twenty feet high, a sort of standard fiery cross height I'd have guessed, and as luminous as the dull

77

yellow street lights along that stretch of suburban trunk road.

I stopped. Well you do, don't you? When you're walking along, slightly drunk but by no means incapable, on a major day of Christian celebration and a red cross fires itself up the sky, you stop. It doesn't matter if you're Christian or not, or whether you're the sort of person whose religious affiliation, at that age, takes a couple of sentences to describe in full, given all the qualifiers which have become attached to it over the years. You stop. I don't believe that if the President of the World Council of Atheists himself was walking along the road and he saw a fiery cross he wouldn't stop for a moment at least, to determine what sort of wind-up he was being subject to.

And me, well, of course I'd stop. I was – am still – an agnostic, and there's nothing more guaranteed to scare an agnostic than a physical manifestation of religious truth. Atheists have got it easy: the idea of a divinity so offends their sense of logic that they get to camp out on the very moral high ground which the religious declare is denied them. But I've never been able to bring myself to deny God's existence: the most I've ever been able to do is to point out that if He does exist it would go against everything else we take for granted about the way that the world and nature works. (And please: I'm not looking for an argument here. Whenever I've written these words or any like them before in public print I get letters and tracts and pamphlets and invitations to visit from those for whom the existence of God is so self-evident they think that it can be demonstrated in a couple of hundred words. I'm not saying you're absolutely wrong and that I'm definitely right, simply that you should save the stamp: there are better marks for your pamphlets, I promise you.)

The problem with agnosticism is that it acknowledges by default that the inexplicable happens, and it's always been my fear that it will happen to me. It's not just fiery crosses, either. I went once to Israel because it seemed so strange to have so many generally antipathetic feelings about the place without having been there, and walked with a friend to the Wailing Wall. I suffered a brief moment of discomfort: what, I thought, if I was suddenly seized upon by an overpowering urge to throw myself down on my knees in front of the wall, ululating away with the men in their black hats, crying for forgiveness or with born-again joy? How would *that* be? I thought.

It didn't happen, because the Wailing Wall turns out to be a big stone wall with people praying and sitting around on old kitchen chairs which have been brought down there over the years and just walking around the place, and I felt as much as I feel at the Tower of London or the Grand Mosque in Istanbul: here I am at a tourist attraction, being a tourist.

The fear is not of sudden faith itself, you understand, because that always seems something of a blessing to those who have it. It's everything which goes with it. It's explaining to my friends that actually, I'm not up for Friday night parties any more. It's that conversation where I say 'honestly you guys – I'm just as much fun as ever I was before, I promise you' and watch their sickly grins because they know I won't laugh next time they tell me who's having an affair with whom and that what's more they won't even try and tell me. It's knowing that if it happened to me I'd have to spread the word, to pass on the good news, to point at passages in the Bible and say. 'Look! Here! It answers that very question! Don't you see?'

And that wasn't the sort of person I particularly wanted to be. Shallow? Of course. Now I live and let live, then I was 17. Even the most pious 17-year-old is shallow. Shallow is what being 17 is for.

Anyway, you can see why a flying fiery cross might cause me to stop.

I tried to work out a rational explanation. At the time I was at the local technical college where a speedfreak called Dawn and her boyfriend spent their weekends in the forest downing pills in cider and building an alien invasion fleet. In fact what they did was to build massive paper balloons out of old copies of the *Walthamstow Guardian* and gum and suspend from them little wire baskets with a stub candle in each. They'd light the candle and as the air inside the balloon heated it would inflate the balloon which would rise into the night sky. Eventually the wind would blow it in such a way that the flame would catch the balloon itself, which would burst into a ball of flame 20 or 30 feet above Epping Forest. They'd phone up the local paper and say they'd seen light in the sky, and when the paper reported it they'd get dozens of other calls from other readers who'd also seen the lights but had been afraid to say anything. Pretty soon the paper balloons started to bring regular visits from the UFO spotters who were convinced that Woodford was ground zero for the alien invasion. Perhaps, I thought, my cross was one of Dawn's inventions.

But no. It was too stable, too bright, had been up there too long already. If it was going to burn itself out it would have done so already. Perhaps, then, it was some sort of luminous kite – but again, no: it was more than luminous, it was alight. And although the light flickered and moved slightly it wasn't with the jerky swaying of a wind-blown kite.

What it was, I decided, was a sign. I ran the last half mile home, threw up, fell into bed, exhausted and slightly perturbed.

When I woke up the next morning the exhaustion had gone, along with the effects of the booze, but the perturbation was still there, although it took me a while – a breakfast, the unwrapping of a couple of Hanukah presents (Hanukah being what we called Christmas in our house), a phone call or two with some of the people I'd been with last night about who'd tried to snog whom and who hadn't stood their round.

But eventually it came back to me: the reason I felt uneasy was because last night I'd seen the light. I laughed: how stupid of me. Surely the cross couldn't have been that large, that long-lasting, that stable. It had to be a plane's landing lights briefly glimpsed in cruciform, or someone having a bonfire on the heath or even, after all, the speedfreaks and their paper balloons rendered spooky by eight pints of gassy beer.

I forgot about it. More or less. But I stayed away from the heath for a while. If Jesus wanted me for a sunbeam he'd have to come and get me somewhere else.

And then a month or so later I found myself walking from Woodford to Buckhurst Hill, a couple of miles to the west. It wasn't until I came up alongside the piece of scrubland that I remembered when I'd last been here. With the lorries and buses roaring past me along the trunk road it felt a less disturbing place than it had that night, and I looked around. Just to my left, twenty yards back from the road where the heath started and a few elderly houses encroached on it was – how could I have never noticed before? – a church. It was an Edwardian building, I imagine, and instead of a steeple it had a steeply pitched roof and presented its gable end towards the road. At the top of the gable end was a cross: a red, neon-lit cross.

It was, as I say, getting on for 30 years ago now, and I may have misremembered. Was it on the gable end or along the front of the church? Did I really run all that way home? Did I stand and watch it for long minutes or see it for a couple of seconds before I started running?

It doesn't matter: I'll stand by the basic elements of the story. The point being? I was a sceptic then and am one still and as a sceptic I know just how much believers in the paranormal are capable of kidding themselves. Leave a true believer alone with a flashing light for a couple of seconds and soon it will be a UFO and then two and then a whole sky full of inexplicably flashing lights. But sceptics kid themselves no more or less than do believers. Had I been ripe for conversion I would have allowed my subconscious to have worked the apparition into a fully-fledged story of angels and ethereal music; as a sceptic I let my mind downgrade the whole event into one I could explain away. There couldn't have been a fiery cross in the sky that Christmas Eve and so in my sceptical mind there wasn't.

Except that's just what there was. I really did see the light.

Diamond's latest book,
*C: Because Cowards Get Cancer Too,*
is published by Vermilion.

# Julie Burchill

## BORN WORKING CLASS

*I have been racking my brains for an idea for this book to raise money for the Medical Foundation Caring for Victims of Torture, which is a cause I feel more strongly about than any other. But as you may have noticed, being a ray of light is hardly my speciality. I wrote this piece recently about the joy and relief of being born working class. But reading it I see that even this is threatening at the end!   J.B.*

WHEN I FIRST joined the staff of the *New Musical Express* in 1976, I was just seventeen. As teenagers do the world over, I loved soft drinks. My drink of choice was that highly-hued non specifically fruit-flavoured symphony of fizz, Tizer. I liked it a) because my grandmother had doled it out like mother's milk but mostly b) because it was SO DAMN TASTY!

Yet whenever I would pop a can of the luscious brew, one of my colleagues would inevitably look up from writing his Jethro Tull review (it was only 1976, after all, and the middle classes always take a while to catch on) and exclaim 'Oh, man! Stop flexing your ROOTS!'

From the word go, my working-class origins have had the power to delight and horrify in equal parts in this wonderful world of the media where I found myself at such a tender age. Up until that point, it is fair to say that I had not known one person who was not working class, with the exception of my schoolteachers. Suddenly, I knew nothing but. Drug-sniffing and joint-rolling they may have been, but middle-class they undoubtedly were They called dinner lunch and tea dinner; always a dead giveaway. I met only one other person from my side of the tracks during my first years there, and in some sort of Darwinist hissy fit I married him.

Yet despite this marital disaster, I still cannot help but feel that, if you *really* want to give a child the best start in life, you will ensure that he or she is working class. Because only someone who starts out working class – right back there on the subterranean starting line – has the potential to be a real success. It's easy to achieve something in life with education, socialization and connections moving you along the inside track; but to make it from nothing, that's *really* something.

A part of me knows that it is silly and snobbish to feel this way, and that people can't help where they're born. But hell, another part of me says that since time immemorial my kind have been exploited and worked into an early grave by those with the upper hand, and that the luxury of feeling smug and superior at having made it *anyway* is the least I'm owed. I know that I may take it too far, in that sometimes I consider only the working class to be *fully human* and therefore worthy of respect, but old Etonians, men, Moslems and residents of Hampstead do this every day. If anyone has the right to be cliquey and chippy, it's the working class.

It just sounds so cool, too. *Working class*; the others just sound so naff. Lower-middle is the one everyone gets embarrassed about, but upper-middle and plain middle seem pretty pathetic to me, too. The upper class are just too few and thick to even bother loathing, and besides, whenever I've had upper-class friends they can't get drunk without insisting that *we* of the upper and working class are the same, yah?, because we just want to get blotto and play with the dog and have a good time, whereas it's the men in the middle who are the enemy; over-educated, tight with money and stiff in all the wrong places.

Middle-class taste is deadening and dull; it has inspired the heavy hand of conformity which makes Tesco sell the same same stuff as Waitrose and makes a plain white-bread cheese sandwich, unsoiled by vegetation or wheatgerm, impossible to buy on the nation's railways. We now have a new edition of the *Communist Manifesto* whose design is approved by Terence Conran, and a leader of the Labour Party who knows the Conran restaurants like the back of his hand but has probably never set foot in a Wimpy Bar. We have choice, we are repeatedly told; but it is a choice pre- packaged for us, the choice to live like a bland, gutless, soft-handed middle-class nonce who has never done an honest day's work in his life, to like the things he likes, to buy the things he buys. But believe it or not, there are some of us who don't want to be Tony Blair when we grow up.

There are some of us who don't want to be middle class because we feel that our own class has, whether through genetics or through necessity, developed more than its fair share of generosity, compassion and good humour. For some strange reason, we don't want to be po-faced car-washers saving our pennies for a rainy day. I, especially, do not and have never wanted to be a middle-class woman, with all the neuroticism, insecurity and sheer stuffiness that the phrase conjures up. With a selection of role models from Barbara Castle to Geri Halliwell to look up to, I can see nothing about women not of my class that I find at all attractive. The one girl I ever fancied, though from a rich family, comes from a pure proletarian bloodline and speaks like a drunken parrot.

If classlessness means the end of inequality, with no private education and no inheritance of either money or property, I'm all for it. If it means, as I feel it does, business as usual on these fronts but the working class being conned into believing that they are no longer being exploited by those who hire their labour, forget it. I picked my team a long time ago, and I'm sticking with it. For, sooner or later, by fair means or foul, we will – as Kruschev said – bury you.

Julie Burchill's autobiography,
*I Knew I Was Right*, is
published by Heinemann.

# Harold Pinter

## JOSEPH BREARLEY 1909–1977
### (Teacher of English)

Dear Joe I'd like to walk with you,
From Clapton Pond to Stamford Hill,
And on
Through Manor House to Finsbury Park.
And back,
On the dead 653 trolleybus,
To Clapton Pond,
And walk across the shadows on to Hackney Downs,
And stop by the old bandstand,
You tall in moonlight,
And the quickness in which it all happened,
And the quick shadow in which it persists.

You're gone. I'm at your side,
Walking with you from Clapton Pond to Finsbury Park,
And on, and on.

# Victoria Glendinning

## SUNSET, SUNRISE

ELLIE LIKED SITTING at the window of her room at Mallory House in the long evenings. She was too high up in the building to look at the shaded back garden without leaning out. What she did see in the slanting sunlight were the rose-filled gardens of the next street, and the tops of the chestnut trees in the park beyond. Her room, east-facing, was in the evenings a cave from which she looked out on to a gilded world.

Tonight Ellie was going out herself. She laid her two best dresses out on the bed. The blue and green flowery silk was twenty years old, but she had always felt nice in it. The other was made of one of those modern materials you can wash, with a pattern of coffee-coloured swirls on white. Ellie twitched the fabrics, looked from one frock to the other, glanced at her clock. Mark was coming at eight.

'I'm just calling to say happy birthday, Aunt Ellie,' Mark had said on the telephone from his office. 'It's some time around now, surely?'

Mark, right now, was scared of having too much to do at work, and of not being able to do it. He was equally scared of having too little to do, which would mean he was not in favour with the chairman any more. No one had come into his office all morning and there hadn't been many internal e-mails either. Yet he had plenty to do. There was a pile of papers on his desk that he absolutely had to get under his belt before the meeting if he was to keep his end up. His stomach churning, he did what he had always done when he was feeling down. He rang his Aunt Ellie. He had reason to do so, today, because of the birthday.

'Yes, the twenty-fourth,' said Ellie. 'Midsummer Day. How clever of you to remember, darling.'

There was a brief silence. Mark, while they were talking, had picked up Courtfield's report on the Glasgow project, and with his free hand began highlighting key phrases, querying Courtfield's dodgy figures, noting with a sickening lurch of the heart that his own name wasn't mentioned once in the text. Bloody Courtfield.

'How could I possibly forget?' he said to Ellie.

'I'll be ninety,' said Ellie. 'Ninety. Isn't that strange. Where has all the time gone?'

Mark abandoned the report. 'Good God, ninety! I don't believe it. This calls for a massive celebration. Let me just look at my book . . . The twenty-fourth is Thursday, right? We'll take you out to dinner, Gail and me. How about the Mitre at Hampton Court? Handy for all of us. We'll pick you up. I'll book a table on the river.'

That was on the Monday. In the intervening days Ellie thought a lot about Mark, her beloved godson, her younger sister Anne's child. But a middle-aged man now of course, I have to remember that. He is such a dear godson. I suppose I always fancied being his fairy godmother. There was that time, when Anne was going through her bad patch, when really I thought of Mark as my own child – all nonsense of course, but harmless surely. It's nice to think how pleased he will be when I've gone. Not that I've got much. The silver teaspoons are good though. I must tell him where my will is, when I see him. Such a *boy*. Anyone under about sixty-five seems young to me.

On the Thursday morning Ellie went to the beauty parlour on the corner and had her hair done, and a manicure. On impulse, she asked for red nail varnish. She hadn't done that for years.

'I'm going out tonight,' she told the manicurist.

'That's nice,' said the girl. She wasn't really interested so Ellie fell silent.

In the afternoon, she rested. I want to be pretty for Mark – and for Gail, I'm never quite sure about Gail. A bit brisk. And always those trouser suits. Maybe she has unfortunate legs. Oh my lovely ankles. Maurice used to call them his filly's fetlocks. I hate it now when they swell up. I don't think she looks after Mark properly either. Of course it doesn't matter, these days, that they aren't married, but it does make you wonder. They've been together for years. At least they don't live together, like so many of the young people I hear of.

Gail and Mark hardly saw one another between Monday and Thursday. They were both frantically busy. She wasn't even in when he got home seriously late on Monday. He rang her with his third Scotch, and left a message. He went round to her place in Kingston for a drink on Tuesday evening, before driving into town to his business dinner for McMaster Lloyd at the new Mirabelle. (Not bad at all.) Gail had seemed a bit tense and ratty. No suggestion of bed, not even a cuddle. There wasn't time, anyway. She was out of town doing a presentation all Wednesday, and stayed in a hotel. But he'd pinned her down for Thursday night at the Mitre. He didn't say the dinner was really for Ellie, for fear that Gail would say, oh, in that case she'd give it a miss if he didn't mind. Ellie was just a boring old bag as far as Gail was concerned, though Gail was very good and always sweet as could be with her. Mark knew he should see Ellie more often, he was all she had left.

Ellie decided on the blue and green floral. She had a nice bath with a gin and tonic, and dressed slowly, because she had a bad dizzy turn when she got out of the bath – not frightening enough to ring the alarm bell provided for the residents of Mallory House, but worse than the last one. Just one of the silly things about being old.

She was ready by a quarter to eight: pearl stud earrings, a squirt of Arpège on her throat, her velvet coat ready to pick up as soon as Mark came for her, and the beaded evening bag holding a handkerchief and the keys to Mallory House and to her room. All ready, she sat again by the window and looked out at the golden treetops. How lucky she was, to be going out with the young people on her ninetieth birthday.

Mark picked Gail up at her office in Surbiton – late, because his five o'clock meeting had gone on for over two hours. He could tell something was wrong with Gail from the way she sat stiffly in the car staring straight in front of her. She came out with it soon enough.

'Jack O'Connell's being transferred to the New York office. From the end of the month.'

Jack O'Connell was Gail's immediate boss. She owed her position in the department entirely to his influence, or so she said.

'It's about the worst thing that could happen, for me.'

As Mark drove, stop-start through the clotted evening traffic, Gail talked. Mark, suppressing his own anxieties about the Components Division, which he had wanted to unload on her, responded with knowing grunts and the odd sharp question.

It boiled down to this: Gail might lose her job altogether. Or she might cling on to it, and be humiliatingly sidelined by Jack's successor – possibly according to office rumour, that guy from the Brussels office who did not like Gail. Or else an outsider, headhunted, in which case he'd bring in his own team, or want to appoint his own people, who might not include her.

'But it's just possible,' she said, 'just *possible*, that Jack will apply for me to go with him to the New York office.'

She said it offhandedly. Too offhandedly. It was her bottom line, everything else had been leading up to it. A red light flared in Mark's mind.

'Has Jack spoken to you about this?'

'He's asked to see me next Tuesday.'

'And if you bugger off to New York, where does that leave me? Where does that leave *us*? Bloody Jack O'Connell. I've got problems of my own, you know. Not that you'd want to hear about them right now I *don't* suppose.'

He needed Gail's sympathetic attention badly. Courtfield wanted him off the Glasgow job. That had been all too obvious at the board meeting. And the chairman hadn't supported Mark over the figures, which were clearly wrong. Courtfield's complacent smile, as he stacked his papers at the end, had been chilling. Mark knew he'd taken a hit, and now saw himself dumped by Gail as well. For of course she would jump at the chance of New York.

'I'm sure you've got problems, Mark,' said Gail icily. 'It's funny, isn't it, whenever I have troubles you always manage to turn the conversation round so that within five minutes we are talking about wonderful important *you* again. As usual.'

Ellie was not really worried when eight o'clock turned into eight-thirty and there was still no sign of Mark. He works very hard, poor boy. He's probably been kept late at the office. Men often are. Though Maurice would always ring up, he was very good that way. She unclipped her pearl studs. They pinched her ear-lobes. She kicked off her navy court shoes. They pinched her bunions. She felt rather sick and faint again, but it was probably just hunger. She was used to having her bit of supper very early, to get it over with. She closed her eyes for a moment.

By the time they walked into the Mitre, Gail and Mark were in the throes of a flaming row from which there was no possible retreat. Mark barked his name at the maitre d', and when they were shown to their table he didn't even hear the gentle question about whether they would like a drink 'while they were waiting'. It was make or break time for him and Gail. She knew it too. She was snarling – like an animal, he thought.

They ordered without caring what they ate, and not caring what damage they did as the pent-up fears, dissatisfactions, resentments, hurts, came pouring out out of their mouths. They were used to suppressing these things, and to cherishing one another's loving, positive qualities. They had prided themselves on not having the petty squabbles other couples went in for. Now his selfishness, her bitchiness, his failure to commit, her deviousness, were adumbrated and condemned in harsh, muffled monotones – for they were in public, they must keep their voices down – and the accusations, and the recalling of unforgotten remarks and incidents, seemed even more cruel because expressed in low, deliberately dispassionate tones.

Ellie woke up in her chair at half-past ten. The sun had gone down, her room was dark. She rose stiffly and put a light on. It hurt her eyes. She did not feel well at all. Then she remembered,. She rang Mark's number, and got his answering-machine voice.

'It's Ellie,' she said to the machine. 'I was just wondering . . . I hope you are all right, my darling. It doesn't matter.'

She thought she would make some cocoa. As she picked up the opened carton of milk from the fridge, she thought how awful it would be if it slipped from her hand and the milk went all over the floor.

The carton slipped from her hand and the milk went all over the floor. Ellie looked at it. She did not have the energy to get down and wipe it up. She did not have the energy to take off her dress, and her underclothes, and put on her nightie. So she sat down again in the chair by the window and looked out at the dark. I think I may have wasted my life. I did not do enough. All those years of tidying the sitting-room and waiting for Maurice to come home. But that's how he wanted it to be, and I did love him. And then all those years of tidying the sitting-room and no Maurice to come home.

She did not even think, if only we had had children, it would have been all right. That worst of all thoughts was worn out, worn through, the unbearable pain of it exhausted. 'I hope you are all right, my darling,' she said to Maurice, into the dark of the night outside her window. 'It doesn't matter.'

Mark and Gail had said all they had to say to each other. They were exhausted. They were frightened. It was late. They were the last diners in the room. The waiter lingered, wanting them to move. They each put a credit card down on the plate: splitting the bill, as they always had done. Never again. It was over. Everything was over.

'So what now?' said Gail in a dead voice, as they walked back to Mark's car.

Maybe it was the familiar sight of their two credit cards slipping across one another on the plate, like emblems of their companionship. Maybe it was the unfamiliar sensation of being in Gail's company with nothing that he had ever thought about himself and her remaining unsaid. Whatever it was, Mark found himself saying, out of a surprising, deep well of security, 'Your place or mine? Mine, I think.'

There was a moment's pause.

'Yes', she said. 'Yes please. Yes.'

And they drove off without speaking much at first, while hope, and longing, and excitement grew in each of their hearts.

Ellie, in her chair in the dark, thought about the first holiday she and Maurice had had in the south of France after the war, when there was nothing for dinner in the restaurants but eggs, melons, tomatoes and small, green grapes; and of the stark shadows cast by olive trees and vines on the hillsides in the ultra-clear evening sunlight, and the black cypresses in the hotel garden, and the cool, dark bedroom with the grey shutters and the red geranium on the window-sill; and the man beside her, waking her in the dawn. Memory became dream, and dream – always this same dream – became something for which there is no name, since the one who experiences it is no longer interested in names and explanations but is willingly drawn in deeper and deeper and further, and away.

'We are living our lives wrong,' said Mark, in the car, as they crossed the river. 'It shouldn't *be* like this. Never having any time, terrified of whatever happens at the office, making work the be all and end all. I mean, what does it really matter how I stand in the Components Division, or how the Components Division stands in the market?'

'Trouble is,' said Gail, 'that we have to do something, if we want to stay alive, and feel alive. We're programmed for economic activity. The barter of goods, or of labour. Hunter-gathering, at the very least.'

'But you and I, in this country at the end of the twentieth century, can hardly start being subsistence farmers.'

'People do.'

'Drop-outs. We aren't cut out to be drop-outs.'

'We'll think of something. We'll start right from the beginning and rethink our lives. We'll have a board-meeting about it.'

'Not tonight.'

'But soon.'

'Just so long as we are in it together.'

'We are together, we shall always be together,' said Gail.

Mark parked the car in a space miraculously and unprecedentedly free right outside his house, and breathed deeply with relief and contentment.

'You go up,' he said in the hallway. 'I'll just check the messages.'

And then: 'Oh God, Ellie . . . Oh God. Too late to ring now. Or too early. It's tomorrow. Oh God. I must make it up to her somehow.' Too tired to feel the full enormity of his forgetfulness, he stumbled up towards his love and his future.

The sun rose behind the chestnut trees in the park, silhouetting their leafy tops against a golden sky, pouring its filtered rays on to the back of Mallory House and into the high open window of Ellie's room. The sun shone on Ellie in her blue and green silk dress, upright in her chair. The sun glinted off her scarlet fingernails and gilded her quiet face. Ellie had made her escape and was one with the glory of the morning. No one knew, no one saw. The telephone rang unanswered at intervals. The administration of Mallory House being rather lax, her departure, or death as it is called, was not discovered until evening, when the sun was going down, and Ellie's room was almost dark again.

Victoria Glendinning's latest book, *Jonathan Swift*, is published by Hutchinson.

# Lana Citron

## THE KISS HOARDER

IT HAPPENED UNEXPECTEDLY and quite unconsciously for she did not stop nor even slow down but continued in her haste towards a certain future. It happened as she walked along a rich road of white stucco houses fronted by bay windows and wide pavements. A moment occurring seemingly unmarked, though telling all the same.

It was early morning, weak heat and she was warming up to a summer alone, a long dried out period of oneness. She had in her mind a residue of feeling and played with it, humming a happiness that was forced, mind over matter, though she did not mind too much and she was thinking how sad it was that some people saved pennies for a rainy day. Jars of copper security whereas she kept kisses. Kisses, now that is real romance. Jars full of kisses, sweet-toothed madness for the excesses which she was loath to waste, which had to be saved at all costs, entailing continuous shop stops to jam jar stock up.

Her tongue was quite stained and she had existed on a diet of syruped bread for over a year. One of her teeth turned brown and another fell out. Such things to her were inconveniences, to lose a tooth was merely a bad dream but to fritter away a kiss constituted something almost catastrophic.

In the blue light of every evening she would rush home carrying a bag containing jam jars and a small loaf of bread which she consumed with relish in the belief she was feeding an appetite to whet her passion. And after she had eaten and wiped the crumbs from her mouth she would deftly and tenderly trace her fingers over her lips. To then purse, pause, pucker and again, and until the vessel cupped in her hands was full to overflowing. Each jar was dated in red ink, grease proof paper under the lid held tight by an elastic band and she kept a log book categorizing every kiss on its intensity, lasting value, quality and depth of passion. And though it was a one-sided affair there were many different types to account for: raindrop kisses that dazzled on a face to be half caught by an open mouth soft wetting the side, downpour kisses, jungle wet and warm, desert kisses parched and dangerous, sun scorched, wind burnt or butterfly ones tongue fluttering. She knew them all and if she didn't she made them up, rapid waterfall kisses, stuttering shy lip trips, blood red biting, valley wide even vomit kisses that splurge out, that shake your insides so. And all kept bottled up until eventually every inch of space was taken over by jar upon jar, piled up any which way.

On reflection it was insane for she had created her own glass ceiling and backed into a corner she realised it was time to get out.

Shaking with the thought of abandoning every kiss caught, the only possessions she had ever truly owned, she was forced to tunnel from beneath her home into the outside world and she found herself where we left her walking along an avenue of maple trees and large windows with visions of homes inside. The summer morning sun was washing over her chapped and swollen mouth easing the muscles of her face. Downhearted she passed a woman proudly pram-pushing her newly born and a young man pulling furiously on the end of cigarette gasping his way to work. Nearby an elderly gent was bent over, having spotted a penny on the pavement and a girl on a bicycle whizzed by. Seemingly oblivious to all of this she walked onward, her pace erratic and her mind absorbed when out of the blue, her right arm darted away from her body and her palm clutched at air, as if physically expecting a stranger palm to join it. It was a sad day, sun sad and the edges of her eyes moistened as tiny tears glimmered in the light.

Lana Citron's first novel, *Sucker*, is published by Secker & Warburg.

# Nicholas Allan

## A QUIET CHRISTMAS . . .

We were planning on a quiet Christmas this year . . . getting away from it all . . . booking into a small hotel perhaps . . .

Nicholas Allan is the author of several children's books, including *Jesus' Day Off* and *Heaven*, published by Hutchinson.

# Acknowledgements

THE PUBLISHERS gratefully acknowledge permission from the following to reprint stories, poems or extracts from work in copyright and to print previously unpublished material:

Nicholas Allan for 'Nativity Game' and 'We Were Planning on a Quiet Christmas' © Nicholas Allan 1998. Louis de Bernières for 'Our Lady of Beauty' © Louis de Bernières 1998. Julie Burchill for 'Born Working Class' © Julie Burchill 1998. Lana Citron for 'The Kiss Hoarder' © Lana Citron 1998. Seamus Deane for 'Carole Dreams of the Wizard' © Seamus Deane 1998. John Diamond for 'Lit Up' © John Diamond 1998. Victoria Glendinning for 'Sunset, Sunrise' © Victoria Glendinning 1998. Charles Handy for 'A Taste of the Sublime' from *The Hungry Spirit* © Charles Handy 1997, published by Arrow. Brian Keenan for an extract from a novel in progress © Brian Keenan 1998. Leslie Kenton for 'Child of Light' © Leslie Kenton 1998. Nigella Lawson for 'Food for the Festival of Lights' © Nigella Lawson 1998. Harold Pinter for 'Joseph Brearley 1909-1977', first published in the *Observer* on 29 November 1987 and subsequently in *Collected Poems and Prose* © Harold Pinter 1991, published by Faber and Faber. Rose Tremain for 'The Candle Maker' from *Evangelista's Fan and Other Stories* © Rose Tremain 1994, published by Sinclair-Stevenson. Marina Warner for 'Necessary Angels' © Marina Warner 1998. Alison Weir for 'Christmas at the Court of Henry VIII' © Alison Weir 1998. Sara Wheeler for 'Camping in Antarctica' from *Terra Incognita* © Sara Wheeler 1996, published by Vintage. Frances Wilks for 'A Light Christmas' © Frances Wilks 1998.

*Caring for victims of torture*

**MEDICAL FOUNDATION**

**Please become a Supporter: Supporters receive
our newsletter three times a year.**

Please return to: The Medical Foundation, FREEPOST,
Star House, 104-108 Grafton Road, London NW5 3YP
Telephone 0171 813 9999 Registered Charity No. 1000340

Name _____

Address _____

_____

_____

Postcode _____

Telephone _____

I would like to make a donation of:

£250     £100     £60     £40     £15

Other

**Method of payment**

I enclose a cheque/postal order made payable
to the Medical Foundation

**Please debit my**

VISA debit card     Master Card     Access
American Express     CAF Charity Card     Visa

Card No. _____

Expiry date _____

Signature _____ Date _____
Please note we are unable to accept Switch debit cards

To make a telephone donation by credit card, please ring
**0800 068 7112**

If you do not require an acknowledgement of your
donation, please tick this box ☐
**Please send me more information on:**
Making a legacy
Gift Aid (for donations of £250 and above)

# Your covenant form

**To make a covenant to the Medical Foundation please complete both forms and return.**

### Tax recovery form (Deed of Covenant)

**Your Name** I (title) _____ (InItials) _____ (surname) _____

**Your Address** Of (address)_____

_____

_____Postcode _____

covenant to the Medical Foundation for the Care of Victims of Torture each year until such a time as I give in notice in writing and in any case for a minimum period of 4 years from the date hereunder (or during my lifetime if shorter) a sum which after deduction of income tax at the basic rate being in force at the time of payment to (net yearly amount you are giving)

£_____

**Todays Date** Dated _____

**Your Signature** Signed and delivered by me _____

**Friend/** In the presence of _____
**Neighbour or**
**Relative** Witness's name _____

**Their Address** Witness's address _____

_____

### Banker's order form

**Your Name** Name _____

**Your Address** Address _____

_____

_____Postcode _____

Please pay to the Medical Foundation Account No. 04877608 at the National Westminster Bank 60-11-30, 92 High Street, Huntingdon each year/quarter/month

£_____

(For office use only)

Quoting Reference No.                              19

**Date you wish** Starting on _____
**to start payment**
Signed _____
To the Manager (please fill in your bank details below)

Name of Bank _____

Bank Address _____

Account No. _____

Sort Code _____

If this instruction cancels all existing banker's orders to the Medical Foundation please tick this box ☐

Thank you for signing these forms. They will enable the Medical Foundation to recover any income tax you have already paid. If you have any questions on completing any aspect of these forms please call 0171 813 9999. Please return this form to the Medical Foundation, not your bank.

101